The Nova Scotia Inns and Restaurants Cookbook

The Nova Scotia Inns and Restaurants Cookbook

Virginia Lee and Elaine Elliot

Formac Publishing Company Limited
Halifax 1985

ISBN 0-88780-055-6 spiral

Cover design: David Howells
Cover illustration: Elizabeth Owen

Canadian Cataloguing in Publication Data

Lee, Virginia, 1947 –
  The Nova Scotia inns and restaurants cookbook

Includes index.
ISBN 0-88780-055-6

1. Cookery, Canadian – Nova Scotia. * 2. Restaurants, lunch rooms, etc. – Nova Scotia. 3. Hotels, taverns, etc. – Nova Scotia. 4. Nova Scotia – Description and travel – 1981–   – Guidebooks. * I. Elliot, Elaine, 1939–
II. Title.

TX715.L43 1985   641.5'09716   C85-098574-9

Formac Publishing Company Limited
5359 Inglis Street
Halifax, Nova Scotia B3H 1J4

Printed and bound in Canada

Contents

This book is dedicated to our mother, Margaret Stuart, a great Nova Scotian cook.

Introduction

Nova Scotia has long had a reputation of warm hospitality and fine traditional cooks. It is our desire to encourage and acknowledge those professionals in the hospitality trade who are endeavoring to maintain and further that reputation.

Many cultures have influenced our cuisine: Scots, Germans, Acadians, Loyalists, etc., and we have tried to offer a variety of fare representative of them. In our research it became evident that available seafood and produce were used astutely, and we found numerous ways of preparing lobster, scallops, apples and root vegetables. We have tested each recipe and adjusted as necessary and have provided both metric and imperial measurements.

We would like to acknowledge the encouragement and support we received from our husbands and families, Rose Marie MacNeil, our French consultant, and our many contributors who took valuable time to send recipes and information about their establishments.

This book is not intended to be a guide to inns and restaurants, but merely to offer a sampling of the fare that is available throughout our province. If you are a native Nova Scotian, please use this book with pride. If you are a visitor, may we offer the Gaelic farewell, "Will ye no come back again".

APPETIZERS

Scallops Sauce Verte
Blomidon Inn

1/2 cup dry vermouth	125 mL
1/2 onion, chopped	1/2
1 sprig fresh parsley	1
1 bay leaf	1
Salt and pepper to taste	
1 lb scallops	500 g
3/4 cup vinaigrette (recipe follows)	175 mL
1/4 cup each of parsley, chives and fresh green of choice, all finely chopped	50 mL
1/3 cup spinach, chopped	75 mL
1 tbsp fresh dill	15 mL

Gently bring vermouth to a simmer. Add onion, sprig of parsley, bay leaf, salt and pepper. Poach the scallops for 3 minutes. Drain and cool, saving the liquid.

Blend vinaigrette with parsley, chives, green of choice, spinach and dill. Thin with up to 1/4 cup (50 mL) of the cooled scallop liquid. Marinate scallops in this mixture for a few hours and serve on a bed of greens with lemon wedges and a sprig of fresh dill or parsley. Serves 4.

Vinaigrette — supplied by authors:	
Combine in a small bowl	
1/4 tsp each of salt and pepper	1 mL
1 1/2 tbsp each of oil and vinegar	25 mL
Beat with a whisk and then add	
3 tbsp oil	45 mL
Beat again and then add	
1 1/2 tbsp vinegar	25 mL
4 1/2 tbsp oil	75 mL
Beat again and store in refrigerator. Makes 3/4 cup (175 mL).	

Stuffed Clams in the Half Shell
Lobster Treat

1 tbsp garlic butter	15 mL
1/4 cup celery, finely minced	50 mL
1/4 cup onion, finely minced	50 mL
1 tbsp green pepper, finely minced	15 mL
2/3 cup unsalted crackers, crumbled	150 mL
1 6-oz (150-g) can baby clams, drained and coarsely chopped	1
1 tbsp fresh lemon juice	15 mL
3 tbsp dry white wine	45 mL
Salt and pepper to taste	

Heat garlic butter in a saucepan and gently cook celery, onion and green pepper until almost fully cooked. Set aside. In a bowl mix crackers, clams, lemon juice and wine. Gently mix in vegetables. Add salt and pepper to taste.

Divide mixture into precleaned clam shells. Cook under the broiler until medium brown. Serve on a bed of lettuce and garnish with parsley. Serves 4.

Savoury Cheese Puffs
Silver Spoon Savouries & Desserts

Pastry:

2 cups flour	500 mL
1/4 tsp salt	1 mL
1 cup butter, chilled and cut in pieces	250mL
1 egg yolk	1
1/2 cup sour cream	125 mL

Spinach Cheese Filling:

1 10-oz (300-g) package of frozen spinach, finely chopped	1
1/2 cup yellow onion, finely chopped	125 mL
1 tbsp vegetable oil	15 mL
Grating of fresh nutmeg	Grating
Pinch of salt and pepper	Pinch
1/2 cup fresh dill, mint or parsley, finely chopped	125 mL
1/3 cup ricotta or cream cheese	75 mL
1/4 cup feta or cream cheese	50 mL

To prepare pastry, combine flour and salt. Cut in butter, a few pieces at a time, until mealy. Add egg yolk and then stir in the sour cream. Chill well and roll out. Cut in 2-inch (5-cm) squares.

To prepare filling, defrost spinach and squeeze out the moisture. Set aside. Cook the onion in oil over low heat until golden. Add spinach and cook 10 to 15 minutes, until dry. Season with nutmeg, salt and pepper. Cool to room temperature and stir in fresh herbs and cheeses.

Place pastry squares in small muffin tins, dollop filling in pastry, fold pastry corners and pinch to seal. Bake at 375°F (190°C) until golden, approximately 18 minutes.

Country Terrine
Gowrie

1 onion, finely chopped	1
1 garlic clove, crushed	1
2 tbsp butter	30 mL
1 lb lean pork, ground	500 g
3/4 lb lean veal, ground	375 g
2 eggs	2
1/4 cup fresh parsley, chopped	50 mL
1/4 tsp allspice	1 mL
2 tbsp brandy	30 mL
1/2 cup fresh herbs, chopped or 1 tbsp dried	125 mL or 15 mL
6-8 slices bacon	6-8
2 boneless chicken breasts, skinned and cut in strips	2
2 bay leaves	2

Sauté onion and garlic in butter until soft. Combine all ingredients, except bacon, chicken and bay leaves, in a large bowl and mix gently. Line a 9″ x 4″ x 3″ (2-L) loaf pan with bacon strips. Pour half the meat mixture in pan and lay strips of chicken down length of pan. Cover with remaining mixture and place bay leaves on top.

Wrap in foil and place in a water bath in a 350°F (180°C) oven for 1 to 1 1/4 hours. Remove from oven, weight top and cool. Refrigerate for 24 hours. Serve thinly sliced on a bed of lettuce accompanied by sour pickles and Melba toast.

Shrimp Louis
The Zwicker Inn

1 cup egg-based mayonnaise	250 mL
1/4 cup heavy cream	50 mL
1/4 cup chili sauce	50 mL
1/4 cup green onion, minced	50 mL
1 1/2 tsp lemon juice	7 mL
Shredded lettuce	
1/2 lb large shrimp, shelled	250 g
1/2 lb baby shrimp	250 g

Blend together mayonnaise, heavy cream, chili sauce, green onion and lemon juice. Spoon sauce on individual beds of shredded lettuce. Embed shrimp in sauce and serve accompanied with thinly sliced radish and cucumber, black olives and hard-boiled egg. Serves 4.

Smokies
The Bright House

2 ripe tomatoes, thinly sliced	2
1/2 lb smoked haddock	250 g
Pepper, freshly ground	
8 tbsp heavy cream	120 mL
Paprika	

Butter well four 1/2-cup ramekins. Divide tomatoes among the dishes. Cover with the smoked haddock, thinly sliced on bias. Sprinkle with freshly ground pepper. Pour 2 tbsp (30 mL) cream over each ramekin and sprinkle with paprika.

Bake at 425°F (220°C) for 15 minutes or until brown and bubbly. Garnish with a lemon wedge. Serves 4.

The chef says that in larger quantities this makes an excellent luncheon dish served with rice and a green salad.

Lemon Steamed Mussels
The Zwicker Inn

3 lb live, cultivated mussels	1.5 kg
6 tbsp unsalted butter	90 mL
2 tbsp flour	30 mL
4 tbsp carrot, grated	60 mL
2 tbsp green onion, chopped	30 mL
2 tbsp parsley, chopped	30 mL
1 garlic clove, minced	1
1/4 tsp pepper	1mL
1/4 cup water	50 mL
20 very thin lemon slices	20

Quickly wash mussels in fresh water, discarding any that are not alive. Combine all ingredients, except mussels, in a large saucepan and bring to a boil, stirring constantly. Add mussels and stir to coat them evenly with sauce. Cover and steam for 3 to 6 minutes, being careful not to overcook.

Remove mussels to 2 large bowls, spoon sauce over shells and serve.

Baked Mushroom Rolls
The Captain's House

1 1/2-2 cups fresh mushrooms, sliced	375-500 mL
1/3 cup butter	75 mL
1/4 cup flour	50 mL
1 cup milk	250 mL
Salt and pepper to taste	
6-8 round bread rolls	6-8

Simmer the mushrooms in half the butter for 5 minutes. Melt remaining butter in a saucepan, add flour and make a roux. Add milk and stir briskly with a whisk until the sauce is thick. Season with salt and pepper. Add the mushroom mixture to the sauce and cook together gently for a few minutes.

Warm the rolls in a 350°F (180°C) oven. When warm, slice open and remove the soft centre. Butter rolls lightly and return to oven. Spoon mixture into rolls and serve. Serves 6 to 8.

SOUPS

Split Pea Soup
Inn Bear River

2 cups split peas	500 mL
Ham bone	
8 cups boiling water	2 L
3-4 garlic cloves, minced	3-4
1 bay leaf	1
3 whole cloves	3
2 tsp salt	10 mL
1 tsp pepper	5 mL
1 cup carrots, chopped	250 mL
1 cup onions, chopped	250 mL

Add split peas and ham bone to boiling water. Turn heat to a simmer. Prepare a bouquet garni with garlic and spices; add to pot. Simmer, covered, for 2 to 3 hours.

Fifteen minutes before serving, remove ham bone from pot and cut small scraps of meat from it. Return meat to the pot and remove spices. Sauté chopped carrots and onions in a little butter until onions are translucent. Add to the soup and continue to cook until vegetables are tender. Serves 8.

Oyster Stew
Highland Heights Inn

2 cups oysters and liquor	500 mL
1/4 cup butter	50 mL
4 cups milk, scalded	1 L
Salt and pepper to taste	

Add oysters and liquor to butter and simmer until their edges begin to curl, about 3 minutes. Scald milk and add oysters and seasonings. Serve immediately. Serves 4 to 6.

Gardener's Vegetable Soup
The Normaway Inn

2 tbsp vegetable oil	30 mL
3/4 cup onions, diced	175 mL
3/4 cup celery with leaves, diced	175 mL
1 clove garlic, crushed	1
1 cup scallions and leeks, sliced	250 mL
1 red or green pepper, diced	1
4 1/2 cups water	1.25 L
1 1/2 tsp salt	7 mL
1/2 tsp basil	2 mL
1/4 cup fresh parsley	50 mL
3/4 cup carrots, diced	175 mL
3/4 cup eggplant, unpeeled and diced	175 mL
3/4 cup butternut squash, unpeeled and diced	175 mL
1/2 cup turnip, peeled and diced	125 mL
3/4 cup potatoes, peeled and diced	175 mL
3/4 cup zucchini, diced	175 mL
1/2 cup string beans, cut	125 mL
1/2 cup lettuce leaves	125 mL
1 cup spinach leaves	250 mL

In oil sauté slowly the onions, celery, garlic, scallions, leeks and red or green pepper for 5 minutes.

Add the water, salt, herbs and remaining vegetables, except lettuce and spinach leaves. Bring to a boil and lower heat to a simmer. Cook, covered, for 45 minutes.

Add lettuce and spinach leaves and cook for another 15 minutes.

This is a very versatile soup, affording many opportunities for substitutions. Greenness and freshness are of the essence.

Chilled Carrot Soup
Garrison House Inn

1 onion, diced	1
4 cloves garlic, crushed	4
2 tbsp butter	30 mL
3 cups small carrots, peeled and chopped	750 mL
4 cups chicken stock	1 L
1 cup orange juice	250 mL
1 cup heavy cream	250 mL
Salt, pepper, cinnamon and nutmeg to taste	

Cook the onion and garlic in butter over low heat. When onion becomes transparent, add carrots and simmer, covered, for 8 to 10 minutes. Add chicken stock and orange juice and bring to a boil. Reduce heat and simmer gently for 30 minutes. Remove from heat, cool slightly and purée in a blender.

In another bowl, lightly whip half of the cream. Gently fold the cream into the soup and add seasonings to taste. Chill for 1 1/2 hours. When serving, add a generous tbsp (15 mL) of cream to each bowl. Serves 6.

Onion Soup
Blue Heron Inn

5 cups onions, thinly sliced	1.25 L
Salt to taste	
6 tbsp butter	90 mL
1/2 tsp dry mustard	2 mL
Dash of thyme	Dash
l qt beef broth	1L
l tbsp tamari (aged soy sauce)	15 mL
3 tbsp dry white wine	45 mL
Dash of pepper	Dash

Cook onions, lightly salted, in butter in a kettle. Cook over medium heat until lightly browned. Add mustard and thyme and mix well. Add remaining ingredients and cook slowly, covered, for at least 30 minutes.

Serve with croutons and grated mozzarella cheese. Serves 4 to 6.

Cream of Leek Soup
Dublin Bay House

2 cups leeks, chopped	500 mL
8 cups rich chicken stock	2 L
5 tbsp butter	75 mL
3 tbsp flour	45 mL
2 tbsp cornstarch	30 mL
2 cups light cream	500 mL
Salt and white pepper to taste	

Wash leeks well to remove sand. Cut off coarse green tops, but retain the last 2 to 3 inches (5 to 8 cm) of tender green along with the white. Chop finely and simmer in stock until tender.

In a separate saucepan melt butter. Add flour and cornstarch. Slowly whisk in light cream and cook over medium heat until thick. Whisking constantly, add cream sauce to stock. Add salt and white pepper to taste. Serves 8.

Curried Corn Chowder
The Whitman Inn

3 tbsp butter	45 mL
2 tsp curry powder	10 mL
1/4 cup green onions, chopped	50 mL
3 1/2 cups canned creamed corn	875 mL
1 cup whole kernel corn	250 mL
3 1/2 cups light cream	875 mL
1/4 tsp ground rosemary	1 mL

Melt butter in a saucepan, add curry powder and cook over low heat for 2 minutes. Sauté green onions until limp, add creamed corn, corn kernels and light cream. Add rosemary and bring to a simmer. Serve garnished with chopped green onions.

Rope Loft Chowder
The Rope Loft

6 medium potatoes, peeled and diced	6
1 small onion, diced	1
2 cups water	500 mL
1 1/2 lb seafood (haddock, scallops, shrimp, lobster)	750 g
2 tsp salt	10 mL
1/2 cup butter	125 mL
2 cups condensed milk	500 mL

Cook potatoes and onion until barely tender in a large pot with 2 cups (500 mL) of water. Add fish and salt and simmer until haddock flakes, about 10 minutes. Add butter and milk, being careful not to let chowder come back to a boil. Serves 4 to 6.

Mussel Soup
The Grand

2 lb mussels	1 kg
1/4 cup shallots, finely chopped	50 mL
1/3 cup onion, finely chopped	75 mL
Few sprigs of parsley and dill	
1/4 bay leaf	1/4
1/2 cup dry white wine	125 mL
1/2 cup celery, in julienne strips	125 mL
1/2 cup carrot, in julienne strips	125 mL
2 tbsp unsalted butter	30 mL
2 cups fish stock	500 mL
3/4 cup heavy cream	175 mL
1 egg yolk, beaten	1
1 tbsp curry powder or to taste	15 mL
Salt and freshly ground pepper to taste	
Pinch of chervil	Pinch

Wash the mussels in cold water, taking care to remove the beards. Place the mussels, shallots, onions, herbs and wine in a covered pot. Bring to a boil, then simmer for 5 minutes. Remove the mussels from their shells and set aside.

Strain the remaining liquid through cheesecloth. In a separate pot, sauté the celery and carrots in butter. Add the fish stock and mussel liquid. Reduce to half, then add the cream. Put the mussels in the soup and remove from heat. Stir a small amount of the hot liquid into the beaten egg yolk; return to the hot mixture. Add curry powder, salt and pepper to taste. Serve hot, garnished with chervil. Serves 4.

SALADS
AND
DRESSINGS

Spinach Salad with Sour Cream Dressing
The Cape House Inn

1/2 cup milk	125 mL
3/4 cup mayonnaise	175 mL
1/2 cup sour cream	125 mL
1/4 cup buttermilk	50 mL
4 1/2 tsp cider vinegar	22 mL
1 1/2 tsp garlic salt	7 mL
1/2 tsp pepper	2 mL
2 tbsp Parmesan cheese, grated	30 mL
Spinach	

Blend together all ingredients, except spinach, and store in refrigerator. Pour dressing to taste over fresh spinach in a bowl. Garnish with grated Swiss cheese, freshly roasted, chopped hazelnuts* and roasted sesame seeds*.

*To roast hazelnuts and sesame seeds, place on a large cookie sheet and bake at 350°F (180°C) for 7 to 10 minutes, until they start to brown.

Waldorf Salad
Boscawen Inn

2/3 cup egg-based mayonnaise	150 mL
1/4 cup sour cream	50 mL
Salt to taste	
4 firm apples, cubed	4
1 stalk celery, thinly sliced	1
1/4 cup raisins	50 mL
1/4 cup walnut halves	50 mL
Lettuce	

Combine mayonnaise, sour cream and salt. Add apples, celery, raisins and walnuts. Mix gently and serve on a bed of lettuce.

Caesar Salad
Garrison House Inn

1 can anchovies, drained	1
1 tbsp Dijon mustard	15 mL
1/3 cup fresh lemon juice	75 mL
6 tbsp olive oil	90 mL
2 garlic cloves, crushed	2
Salt and pepper to taste	
1 large head of romaine lettuce	1
3 tbsp Parmesan cheese	45 mL
1 egg	1
Croutons	

In bottom of a large wooden bowl, crush the drained anchovies. Stir in the mustard, lemon juice, olive oil and crushed garlic cloves. Mix thoroughly and add salt and pepper to taste.

Wash and dry a large head of romaine lettuce. Tear into bite-sized pieces and add to the salad bowl. Sprinkle with Parmesan cheese. Coddle egg for 1 minute and break over salad. Mix gently and add croutons.

Privateers' House Dressing
Upper Deck Restaurant

3/4 cup vegetable oil	175 mL
2 raw egg yolks	2
2 tbsp vinegar	30 mL
1 tsp Dijon mustard	5 mL
2 tbsp red wine	30 mL
2 hard-boiled eggs, finely chopped	2
Salt and pepper to taste	
Pinch of dried tarragon	Pinch

Beat the oil with the raw egg yolks. Add the vinegar, mustard, wine and hard-boiled eggs. Beat mixture for 1 minute and season with salt, pepper and tarragon.

Tangy Old-fashioned Dressing
The Village Estate

1 cup white sugar	250 mL
2 tbsp flour	30 mL
2 tsp dry mustard	10 mL
1 tsp salt	5 mL
1 egg, beaten	1
1 tbsp butter, melted	15 mL
1 cup white vinegar	250 mL
1 cup milk	250 mL

In top of a double boiler, over simmering water, stir together sugar, flour, mustard and salt. Blend in beaten egg and mix well. Stir in melted butter, vinegar and milk, blending until smooth. Cook and stir until thick, 10 to 15 minutes. Let cool; dressing will continue to thicken. Store in a glass jar in refrigerator up to 1 month.

South Shore Dutch Cucumber Salad
Milford House

2 cucumbers, peeled and thinly sliced	2
1 large onion, thinly sliced	1
1 tbsp salt	15 mL
1-2 tbsp vinegar	15-30 mL
1/4 cup cream	50 mL
1/2 cup sugar	125 mL

Layer cucumber and onion slices in a large bowl, sprinkling with salt between layers. Let stand several hours with a weight on top to express juices. Pour off excess brine and rinse well. Combine vinegar, cream and sugar and mix with vegetables. Garnish with parsley or chopped chives.

Honey French Dressing
The Zwicker Inn

1/2 cup honey	125 mL
1/3 cup lemon juice	75 mL
1/2 tsp lemon zest (finely grated peel)	2 mL
3/4 tsp celery seed, crushed	3 mL
1 tsp salt	5 mL
1/2 tsp paprika	2 mL
1/2 tsp dry mustard	2 mL
1/2 tsp pepper, freshly ground	2 mL
3/4 tsp Worcestershire sauce	3 mL
1 cup vegetable oil	250 mL

In a blender or food processor combine all ingredients, except oil. Mix well. Slowly add oil and blend until thick and creamy. Makes 1 2/3 cups (400 mL).

Nancy's Blue Cheese Dressing
The Whitman Inn

1 cup salad oil	250 mL
1/3 cup wine vinegar	75 mL
1/3 cup mayonnaise or sour cream	75 mL
1 tsp salt	5 mL
1 tsp dry mustard	5 mL
3 cloves garlic	3
1/2 tsp pepper	2 mL
1 tbsp Worcestershire sauce	15 mL
1 tbsp tamari sauce	15 mL
1/4 cup blue cheese	50 mL

Mix ingredients together in a blender or food processor until almost smooth.

Rodeau Cabbage Slaw
The Village Estate

1/2 green cabbage, shredded	1/2
1/2 red cabbage, shredded	1/2
1/2 red onion, thinly sliced	1/2
1 green pepper, thinly sliced	1
1 carrot, shredded	1
1 stalk celery, thinly sliced	1

Dressing:	
2 tbsp Dijon mustard	30 mL
1 tsp celery seed	5 mL
1 tsp salt	5 mL
1/2 tsp black pepper	2 mL
1/4 cup sugar	50 mL
2 tbsp lemon juice	30 mL
1/2 cup red wine vinegar	125 mL
3/4 cup vegetable oil	175 mL

Combine vegetables in a large plastic bag.

To prepare dressing, whisk ingredients together until smooth.

Add dressing to vegetables and toss. Press out air and seal with a twist tie. Marinate salad in the refrigerator for 2 to 4 hours, turning the bag several times to mix well.

MEATS
AND
POULTRY

Lamb Brochettes with House Spices
The Pines Resort Hotel

2 cups dry red wine	500 mL
1/4 cup lemon juice	50 mL
1 bay leaf	1
Dash each of ginger and mace	Dash
Pinch each of curry, ground coriander, salt and pepper	Pinch
2 lb lamb, cubed	1 kg
Mushrooms, blanched	
Onions, blanched	

Sauce:	
Marinade from preparation above	
1 cup beef broth	250 mL
1 tbsp butter	15 mL
1 1/2 tbsp flour	22 mL
Salt and pepper to taste	
3 tbsp heavy cream	45 mL

Mix together the wine, lemon juice, bay leaf, spices, salt and pepper. Pour into a glass bowl and marinate the lamb cubes for 18 hours.

Place marinated meat cubes on a skewer and alternate each cube with a blanched mushroom and a blanched onion quarter. Cook to desired doneness on a barbecue or oven broil, turning once. Serve on a bed of curried rice pilaf, accompanied by sauce.

To prepare the sauce, strain the marinade from the lamb cubes. Reduce at medium heat by one-quarter. Add beef broth and reduce again by one-quarter. Knead together butter and flour and form into small balls. Add balls of manipulated butter to boiling sauce, one at a time, stirring constantly, until sauce is thickened to the consistency of a thick table cream. Add salt and pepper to taste. Stir in heavy cream and serve. Serves 4 to 6.

Baked Breast of Chicken South Shore
The Captain's House

4 4-oz (125-g) chicken breasts, boneless	4
1/4 cup flour	50 mL
2 tbsp vegetable oil	30 mL
2 tbsp Dijon mustard	30 mL
Pinch of dried tarragon	Pinch
4 slices lean bacon, partially cooked	4
1 small onion, diced	1
Chicken brown sauce (recipe follows)	
1/4 cup dry white wine	50 mL
Pinch of black pepper	Pinch

Dust chicken breasts lightly with flour and sauté in oil. Remove from pan and coat sparingly with mustard and tarragon. Wrap each breast with a slice of bacon and fasten with a toothpick.

Arrange chicken in a small casserole, add remaining ingredients and bake at 350°F (180°C) for 30 minutes. Garnish with parsley and lemon slices. Serves 4.

Chicken Brown Sauce — supplied by authors:	
1/2 small onion	1/2
1 1/2 tbsp butter	22 mL
1/2 cup dry white wine	125 mL
3/4 cup chicken stock	175 mL
1/2 tsp parsley	2 mL
1/2 bay leaf	1/2
1 tbsp butter	15 mL
1 1/2 tbsp flour	22 mL

Cook onion in butter over medium heat until golden brown. Add wine and stock and bring to a boil. Add parsley and bay leaf and boil briskly until liquid is reduced by one-third. Knead together 1 tbsp (15 mL) butter and 1 1/2 tbsp (22 mL) flour. Form into small balls and add to boiling sauce, one at a time, stirring constantly, until sauce reaches the consistency of heavy cream.

Santa Fe-style Chicken
The Village Estate

3 tbsp oil	45 mL
1/3 cup fresh lime juice	75 mL
1/2 tsp salt	2 mL
1/4 tsp pepper	1 mL
4 large chicken breasts	4
2 cups canned tomatoes	500 mL
1 small onion, diced	1
1 green pepper, diced	1
1 tsp ground coriander	5 mL
2 tbsp red wine vinegar	30 mL
Salt to taste	
1 cup fresh mushrooms, sliced	250 mL
1/4 cup celery, diced	50 mL
1/2 cup sour cream	125 mL

Whisk together oil, lime juice, salt and pepper until blended. Brush chicken breasts with this marinade and broil 4 inches (10 cm) from element or on a barbecue for 10 to 15 minutes, each side, until cooked.

In a saucepan, mix tomatoes, onion, green pepper, coriander, vinegar, salt, mushrooms and celery and bring to a boil. Simmer, stirring occasionally, until mixture is slightly reduced and thickened. Stir in sour cream. Serve sauce over cooked chicken. Serves 4.

Stuffed Pork Tenderloin
Silver Spoon Savouries & Desserts

2 pork tenderloins, about 1 lb (500 g) each	2

Filling:

3 tbsp brandy	45 mL
1/4 cup butter	50 mL
2/3 cup dried apricots, diced	150 mL
2/3 cup dried figs or prunes, diced	150 mL

Brown Sauce:

1 1/2 tbsp butter	22 mL
1/2 small onion, diced	1/2
1/4 cup brandy	50 mL
1 cup beef broth	250 mL
1/2 tsp parsley	2 mL
1/2 bay leaf	1/2
1 tbsp butter	15 mL
1 1/2 tbsp flour	22 mL

Slice tenderloins almost in half to form a pocket for the stuffing. Prepare filling by processing brandy, butter and diced fruit for 2 minutes. Spoon into the two tenderloins and secure with skewers or butcher's twine. Wrap tenderloins in foil and bake in a preheated 375°F (190°C) oven for 30 minutes or until all pink disappears from the meat. Slice and serve with brown sauce. Serves 4 to 6.

To prepare brown sauce, melt 1 1/2 tbsp (22 mL) butter in a saucepan and add diced onion. Cook until onion turns golden brown. Add brandy and beef broth and bring to a boil. Add parsley and bay leaf. Boil briskly until liquid is reduced by one-third. Knead together 1 tbsp (15 mL) butter and 1 1/2 tbsp (22 mL) flour. Form into small balls and add to boiling sauce, one at a time, stirring constantly, until sauce reaches the consistency of heavy cream.

Chicken Crêpes with Orange and Almonds
Boscawen Inn

3 cups cooked chicken, diced	750 mL
1 cup mandarin orange slices	250 mL
1/2 cup almonds, sliced	125 mL
2 cups béchamel sauce with sweet sherry (recipe follows)	500 mL
8 crêpes (see page 78)	8

Combine chicken, oranges, almonds and béchamel sauce and mix well. Heat in saucepan over medium heat until hot. Fill each crêpe with 1/2 cup (125 mL) of mixture. Place on a heated platter and keep warm. Pour remaining sauce over crêpes. Garnish as desired. Serves 4.

Béchamel Sauce — supplied by authors:

4 tbsp butter	60 mL
3 tbsp flour	45 mL
2 cups milk	500 mL
1 tbsp sherry	15 mL
Salt to taste	

Melt butter over low heat. Add flour, a little at a time, and stir for 3 to 4 minutes. Whisk in milk, stirring constantly until thick and smooth. Remove from heat and add sherry and salt to taste. Yields 2 cups.

Roast Leg of Lamb with Sage
Gowrie

1 leg of lamb, with the bone removed	1
2 cloves garlic	2
1/2 tsp rosemary	2 mL
1/2 tsp salt	2 mL
1/4 tsp pepper	1 mL

Stuffing:

1 medium onion, finely chopped	1
2 tbsp butter	30 mL
4 slices bread with crusts	4
4 slices toast	4
1 medium potato, boiled and mashed	1
2 tsp sage	10 mL
1/4 cup fresh parsley, chopped	50 mL
Salt and pepper to taste	

Remove lamb from refrigerator 2 hours before cooking, wipe carefully and rub the surface with a cut clove of garlic. Make a series of small slits in the skin of the lamb and insert slivers of the second garlic clove. Rub roast with rosemary, salt and pepper.

To prepare stuffing, sauté onion in butter until golden. Finely chop bread and toast. Add onion, mashed potato, herbs, salt and pepper. Mix gently and stuff the cavity that was formed when the bone was removed from the lamb. Tie roast with butcher's twine.

Place in a 400°F (200°C) oven for 10 minutes. Reduce heat to 325°F (160°C) and cook until internal temperature of meat is 165°F (75°C), about 1 3/4 to 2 1/2 hours, depending upon the size of the leg. Remove from oven and let set 15 minutes before carving. Serves 6 to 8.

Summer Lamb
Bayberry House

1 tsp each of salt and pepper	5 mL
1 tsp Dijon mustard	5 mL
2 tbsp honey	30 mL
1 tsp dried rosemary, crushed	5 mL
1 tsp mint, chopped	5 mL
1 leg, rack or shoulder of lamb	1
1 cup water	250 mL

Sauce:

1/4 cup red currant jelly	50 mL
1/2 cup orange juice and zest	125 mL
1/4 cup dry white wine	50 mL
1 cup chicken stock	250 mL
2 tbsp mint, finely chopped	30 mL
2 tbsp light cream	30 mL

Mix the salt, pepper, mustard, honey, rosemary and mint and spread over the fat side of the lamb roast. Place the meat on a rack over a shallow roasting pan. Add 1 cup (250 mL) water to the pan. Place in a preheated 325°F (160°C) oven and roast 25 minutes per pound for rare, 28 to 31 minutes for medium and 32 to 35 minutes for well done.

To prepare sauce, heat red currant jelly, orange juice, zest, wine and stock. Cook until reduced to half volume. Add chopped mint and cream.

Roast Beef Wellington
The Cape House Inn

2 tbsp butter	30 mL
2 cups mushrooms, sliced	500 mL
1 tbsp onion, minced	15 mL
1/2 tsp parsley	2 mL
2 cups Swiss cheese, grated	500 mL
3 cups rare roast beef, sliced in thin strips	750 mL
2 tbsp prepared horseradish	30 mL
6 6-inch x 6-inch (10-cm x 10-cm) squares of puff pastry	6
1 egg beaten with 1 tsp water	5 mL

Horseradish Sauce:

1 1/2 cups sour cream	375 mL
1/4 cup prepared horseradish	50 mL
1 clove garlic, minced	1

Melt butter in a large skillet over medium heat and sauté the mushrooms, onion and parsley until tender, about 5 minutes. Remove from heat, cool and drain well.

Grease a large baking sheet. Toss cheese, beef, prepared horseradish and mushroom mixture in a large bowl, blending well. Divide mixture into 6 portions. Spoon 1 of these portions onto the centre of a pastry square. Fold up corners of pastry, pinch to seal, but do not compress filling. Transfer to baking sheet with seam-side down. Repeat for remaining portions and pastry squares. Brush pastry with egg wash. Bake in a preheated 450°F (230°C) oven until puffed and golden, about 25 to 30 minutes.

To prepare horseradish sauce, blend ingredients.

Serve Roast Beef Wellington hot with horseradish sauce on the side.

Chinese Chicken Wings
Inn Bear River

24-32 chicken wings, wing tips removed	24-32
1/2 cup soy sauce	125 mL
1/2 cup brown sugar	125 mL
1/3 cup sherry	75 mL
2 garlic cloves, minced	2
1 tsp oil	5 mL
Hot pepper oil to taste	
1/2 tsp ground ginger	2 mL
1/4 tsp cinnamon	1 mL

Arrange wings in a baking pan. Combine remaining ingredients and pour over wings. Marinate 2 to 8 hours.

Bake at 425°F (220°C) for 40 minutes, basting occasionally. Serves 4.

Marinated Lamb Chops
The Normaway Inn

2 cups canned tomatoes with seeds removed, puréed	500 mL
1/2 cup red wine	125 mL
1 clove garlic, minced	1
1 tsp fresh thyme	5 mL
1 tbsp brown sugar	15 mL
8 loin lamb chops	8
Salt and pepper to taste	

Combine tomatoes, wine, garlic, thyme and sugar. Bring to a boil. Cool and pour over lamb chops and marinate for 3 hours.

Broil 5 inches (10 cm) from the heat for 10 minutes on the first side. Sprinkle with salt and pepper and broil second side for 7 minutes. Serves 4.

Baked Ham Jamicque
O'Carroll's

1 cup dark brown sugar	250 mL
1 tsp ground cloves	5 mL
1 tsp cinnamon	5 mL
6 portions smoked ham, 1/2 inch (1 cm) thick	6
1 pineapple (cut in rings) or 1 19-oz (540 mL) tin pineapple rings (in own syrup), drained	1
1 cup pineapple juice	250 mL
1/4 cup dark rum	50 mL
3 bananas	3

Combine sugar and spices and coat ham slices with three-quarters of the mixture. Lay ham in bottom of greased oven-proof dish. Arrange pineapple rings on ham and sprinkle with remaining sugar mixture. Combine pineapple juice and rum and pour over ham.

Bake, covered, in 350°F (180°C) oven for approximately 30 minutes. Halve bananas and add to baked ham for last 10 minutes of cooking. Serves 6.

Steak and Kidney Pie
The Bright House

3 tbsp drippings	45 mL
1 lb round steak, cubed	500 g
1 lb beef kidney, thinly sliced	500 g
2 medium onions, finely diced	2
2 1/2 cups mushrooms, sliced	625 mL
4 tbsp flour	60 mL
1/2 tsp salt	2 mL
1/4 tsp each of ginger, dry mustard and pepper	1 mL
2 1/2 cups beef stock	625 mL
Pie shell to cover	
1 egg, beaten	1

Melt drippings in a large frying pan, add steak and kidney and brown over medium heat. Add onions and mushrooms and fry for 5 minutes. Stir in flour and seasonings until well blended. Gradually add beef stock. Bring to a boil, cover and simmer very gently until tender, 1 1/2 to 2 hours.

Transfer to a casserole and cool. Roll a pastry to 1/4-inch (6-mm) thickness. Line the edges of the casserole with a 1-inch (2.5-cm) strip of pastry. Dampen edges and cover entire casserole with pastry. Press down firmly on edges, trim and flute. Cut letters "S" and "K" in centre of pastry to allow steam to escape. Brush pastry with a beaten egg.

Bake at 425°F (215°C) for 10 minutes, reduce heat to 375°F (190°C) and continue to bake for about 30 minutes. Serves 4 to 6.

Fillet of Beef Atlantic
Amherst Shore Country Inn

3 tbsp onion, chopped	45 mL
2 tbsp butter	30 mL
4 tbsp flour	60 mL
2 cups light cream	500 mL
6 tbsp consommé	90 mL
1/4 cup dry white wine	50 mL
18 medium shrimps, sliced in half lengthwise	18
18 scallops, sliced in half	18
6 8-oz (250-g) beef tenderloin fillets, 1 1/4 inches (3 cm) thick	6

In a medium skillet sauté onion in butter until slightly browned. Add flour to make a roux. Gradually and carefully add cream, consommé and wine. Cook, stirring constantly, until sauce is the consistency of heavy cream. Add shellfish and keep warm.

Grill or barbecue fillets until desired degree of doneness. Pour 1/2 cup (125 mL) seafood sauce over each fillet. Serve with rice pilaf. Serves 6.

Jack's Glorious Goulash
The Zwicker Inn

1 1/2 lb beef, cubed	750 g
1 medium onion, sliced	1
2 cloves garlic, crushed	2
1 cup canned tomatoes, chopped	250 mL
1 tbsp cider vinegar	15 mL
2 cups water	500 mL
1 tsp paprika	5 mL
1 tbsp tamari	15 mL
1/2 tsp salt	2 mL
1/4 tsp pepper	1 mL
1/2 tsp caraway seeds, crushed	2 mL
1/4 tsp marjoram	1 mL
2 tbsp flour	30 mL
2 cups mushrooms, sliced	500 mL

Place meat, onion, garlic, tomatoes, vinegar, water, paprika and tamari in a large pot and bring to a simmer. Add seasonings and simmer 1 1/2 hours, until meat is fork-tender.

Remove meat from pot and measure volume of juice. Bring to 1 1/3 cups by reducing or adding water. Mix 2 tbsp (30 mL) flour with enough water to make a paste, combine with a bit of the liquid and stir into the pot. Simmer, stirring until thickened. Add the mushrooms and simmer 5 minutes. Return meat to the sauce and bring to serving temperature. Serve over noodles.

Veal with Green Peppercorn and Paprika Sauce
Clipper Cay

1 1/2 lb veal cutlets	750 g
2 tbsp butter	30 mL
5-10 green peppercorns	5-10
1/4 cup white wine	50 mL
1 1/2 cups heavy cream	375 mL
Paprika to colour	

Pound cutlets to 1/8-inch (3-mm) thickness. Sauté in butter until barely done. Remove veal from pan and keep warm. Add peppercorns and deglaze pan with wine. Stir in heavy cream and reduce over medium-high heat to 1 1/4 cups (300 mL). Add paprika to colour.

Return cutlets to sauce and simmer 4 to 5 minutes. Preheat oven to 350°F (180°C) and bake cutlets for 5 minutes. Serve with rice. Serves 4.

Boeuf Stroganoff
O'Carroll's

1 1/4 lb beef fillet	625 g
2 tbsp butter	30 mL
1 medium onion, finely chopped	1
2 cups mushrooms, thinly sliced	500 mL
1 tbsp tomato paste (optional)	15 mL
1 cup beef stock	250 mL
1/2 cup sour cream	125 mL
1 tsp Worcestershire sauce	5 mL
Dash Tabasco sauce	Dash

Slice the fillet across the grain in small, thin strips. Heat butter in a wide pan; when it froths, fry meat until it changes colour. Add onion, mushrooms and tomato paste, if desired. Sauté gently 1 to 2 minutes.

Add as much beef stock as needed to give desired consistency. Bring to a boil and simmer, covered, for 15 minutes. Stir occasionally. Add sour cream and seasonings and reheat gently. Serve with rice. Serves 4.

Cold Chicken Breast with Orange Curry Mayonnaise

The Zwicker Inn

4 cups water	1 L
1 tbsp salt	15 mL
1 1/2 lb boneless chicken breast	750 g

Orange Curry Mayonnaise:	
1 cup egg-based mayonnaise	250 mL
2 tbsp orange juice	30 mL
2 tsp parsley, minced	10 mL
Curry powder to taste	

Bring water and salt to a boil. Add chicken breasts and reduce heat to a simmer. Poach chicken, stirring occasionally, until it is no longer pink when cut in the thickest part. Cool and chill.

Place cold chicken on serving plates, coat generously with Orange Curry Mayonnaise. Garnish with cucumber, orange slices and fresh parsley.

To prepare the Orange Curry Mayonnaise, mix the mayonnaise, orange juice and parsley. Add curry powder to taste. Chill.

SEAFOOD

Poached Salmon
The Normaway Inn

2 cups water	500 mL
1/2 tsp salt	2 mL
1/2 cup white wine	125 mL
1/2 lemon, juice and rind	1/2
1/2 medium onion, studded with 2 whole cloves	1/2
1/2 stalk celery	1/2
1/2 carrot, peeled and sliced	1/2
1/2 bay leaf	1/2
1/2 tsp thyme	2 mL
2 peppercorns	2
4 serving-sized salmon steaks	4

Hollandaise Sauce:	
3 egg yolks	3
1 tbsp cold water	15 mL
1/4 tsp salt	1 mL
Pinch of pepper	Pinch
1 tbsp lemon juice	15 mL
1/4 cup butter, melted	50 mL
1 tsp Dijon mustard (optional)	5 mL

Combine water, salt, wine, juice and rind of half a lemon, vegetables and herbs. Bring to a boil and simmer for 10 minutes. Place salmon in boiling stock and simmer until fish flakes easily when tested with a fork, 8 to 12 minutes. Serve with lemon wedges and hollandaise sauce. Serves 4.

To prepare sauce, in the top of a double boiler, beat egg yolks, water, salt and pepper with a wire whisk until thick. Set over hot (not boiling) water.

Gradually add the lemon juice, while beating constantly. Continue to beat and cook until the sauce is the consistency of thick cream. Remove double boiler from heat, leaving top in place.

Slowly beat melted butter into sauce and continue to mix until it is thoroughly blended. Add Dijon mustard, if desired.

Nova Scotia Lobster in Sweet Cream Sauce
Lobster Treat

1 garlic clove, crushed	1
4 tbsp butter	60 mL
4 tbsp flour	60 mL
1 cup fish stock	250 mL
2 tbsp dry white wine	30 mL
1 cup heavy cream	250 mL
1 lb lobster meat	500 g
Salt and pepper to taste	

Sauté garlic in butter for a few minutes. Whisk in flour to form a roux. Slowly add hot fish stock, stirring constantly. Cook gently for 5 minutes, until smooth and slightly thickened. Stir in the wine. Remove from the heat and whisk in the cream.

Return to serving temperature and fold in the lobster meat. Turn into individual casseroles and let stand 2 to 3 minutes before serving. Season with salt and pepper to taste. Serves 4.

Cioppino
Bayberry House

2 garlic cloves, minced	2
1 cup onion, chopped	250 mL
1 cup green onion, chopped	250 mL
1 green pepper, diced	1
1/4 cup olive or corn oil	50 mL
1 28-oz can of tomatoes	796 mL
1 5 1/2-oz (150-mL) can of tomato paste	1
2 cups fish stock or 1 bottle clam juice plus water to make 2 cups	500 mL
1/4 tsp thyme	1 mL
1 bay leaf	1
1 tbsp grated orange peel	15 mL
2 cups white wine	500 mL
2 lb fish (halibut, sole, scallops), cut in pieces	1 k
1 cooked lobster, cut in pieces	1
1 cup crab meat	250 mL
1 lb shelled raw shrimp	500 g
Salt and pepper to taste	

Sauté garlic, onion, green onion and green pepper in oil until limp. Add the tomatoes, tomato paste, fish stock or clam juice and water, thyme, bay leaf and orange peel. Simmer for 2 hours, until thick. Add the wine and return to a simmer.

About 20 minutes before serving time, add the pieces of fish. Ten minutes prior to serving, add the pieces of lobster, crab meat and raw shrimp. Add salt and pepper to taste.

Serve this rich, meal-in-one soup with hot garlic bread. Serves 6 to 8.

Salmon and Caviar
The Grand

1 lemon	1
2 tbsp butter	30 mL
1 1/4 cup shallots, sliced	300 mL
2 cups mushrooms, sliced	500 mL
1 1/2 lb salmon fillet	700 g
1/2 cup water	125 mL
2/3 cup dry white wine	150 mL
1 1/4 cup heavy cream	300 mL
Salt and pepper to taste	
3 tbsp caviar	45 mL

Peel the lemon and thinly slice the skin. Place peel in a small saucepan, cover with water and boil for 1 minute. Strain and cool.

In a separate skillet, melt the butter and cook the shallots for 6 minutes. Add the mushroom slices and cook for 6 additional minutes, stirring frequently. Add the salmon fillet, water and wine. Poach for 6 minutes.

Place the salmon on a platter and remove the skin with a sharp knife. Keep warm.

To prepare the sauce, add the heavy cream to the skillet and boil until slightly thickened, 2 to 4 minutes.

Remove from heat and add lemon peel. Adjust seasoning with salt and pepper as necessary. Divide salmon into 4 servings, sprinkle with caviar and top with sauce. Serves 4.

Devilled Crab Meat
Dublin Bay House

2/3 cup shallots, finely chopped	150 mL
1 cup mushrooms, sliced	250 mL
5 tbsp butter	75 mL
2 lb crab meat	1 k
2 tbsp parsley, chopped	30 mL
Parmesan cheese, grated	

Cream Sauce:

2 1/2 tbsp butter	35 mL
2 1/2 tbsp flour	35 mL
1 1/2 cup light cream	375 mL
1 tsp dry mustard	5 mL
2 tbsp lemon juice	30 mL
1/2 tsp seasoned salt	2 mL
Dash of cayenne pepper	Dash
Salt and pepper to taste	

Sauté shallots and mushrooms in butter until shallots are clear, but not brown. Add crab meat and remove from heat.

Prepare cream sauce by melting butter in a saucepan over low heat. Add flour to make a roux and whisk in the cream. Stir and cook until thick. Whisk mustard, lemon juice and seasonings into cream sauce. Combine with crab, shallots, mushrooms and parsley, being careful not to break the larger pieces of crab.

Portion into scallop shells or individual ovenproof serving dishes. Top with grated Parmesan cheese. Heat in a 350°F (180°C) oven for 10 to 15 minutes and finish under the broiler until golden brown. Serves 6 to 8.

Scallop Casserole
Milford House

1 lb scallops	500 g
Salt and pepper to taste	
1 cup celery, diced	250 mL
1/2 cup onion, minced	125 mL
1 cup mushrooms, sliced	250 mL
2 tbsp butter	30 mL

White Sauce:	
4 tbsp butter	60 mL
4 tbsp flour	60 mL
2 cups milk	500 mL

Topping:	
1 cup bread crumbs	250 mL
3 tbsp butter, melted	45 mL
1/2 cup cheese, grated	125 mL

Spread scallops on a plate and sprinkle with salt and pepper. Sauté celery, onion and mushrooms in butter until limp, but not brown.

Prepare white sauce by melting butter in a saucepan and slowly whisking in the flour. Gradually stir in the milk and cook over medium heat, stirring constantly until mixture thickens.

Gently combine scallops, vegetables and white sauce. Pour into a buttered casserole and top with the bread crumbs, melted butter and grated cheese. Bake at 375°F (190°C) until brown and bubbly, about 20 minutes. Serves 4.

Noodles with Lobster and Tarragon
Blomidon Inn

1 cup onions, finely chopped	250 mL
4 tbsp olive oil	60 mL
2 cups plum tomatoes, drained and chopped	500 mL
4 tsp dried tarragon	20 mL
Salt and pepper to taste	
2 cups heavy cream	500 mL
Pinch of cayenne pepper	Pinch
1 1/2 lb lobster meat	750 g

Sauté the onions in oil for 20 minutes, being careful not to brown. Add drained tomatoes and tarragon. Bring to a boil and season with salt and pepper. Reduce heat and simmer, covered, for 30 minutes. Let cool and purée in a processor.

Return to a saucepan and add the heavy cream. Simmer until slightly reduced. Add cayenne and lobster meat. Return to serving temperature. Serve over fettuccine or other fine pasta. Garnish with parsley and fresh tarragon. Serves 4.

Fried Clams
Harris' Seafood Restaurant

1 lb shucked clams	500 g
2/3 cup flour	150 mL
1/2 egg	1/2
1 cup milk	250 mL
2 cups fine cracker crumbs	500 mL

Rinse clams and dry between paper towels. Cut away the black skin of the neck. Dredge clams in flour, dip in egg wash (egg and milk beaten together), then dredge in cracker crumbs. Deep-fry at 350°F (180°C) until golden brown and crisp, about 3 to 5 minutes. Serves 4.

Haddock Bonne Femme
The Rope Loft

4 7-oz (220-g) haddock fillets	4
1 small onion, finely chopped	1
3/4 cup mushrooms, chopped	175 mL
1/3 cup white sauterne wine	75 mL
1 cup white sauce (recipe follows)	250 mL

Place fillets in a shallow, greased baking dish. Sprinkle with onion and mushrooms. Pour in the wine and bake at 450°F (220°C) for 7 minutes or until fish flakes easily with a fork.

To serve, top the fillets with warm white sauce to which the pan juices have been added. Garnish with a lemon wedge and paprika. Serves 4.

White Sauce — supplied by authors:	
2 tbsp butter	30 mL
2 tbsp flour	30 mL
1 cup milk	250 mL

Melt butter in a saucepan over low heat. Whisk in the flour and gently stir in the milk. Stir and cook until sauce is the desired thickness.

Lobster Nova Scotia-style
Harris' Seafood Restaurant

4 cups fresh or frozen lobster	1 L
4 tbsp butter	60 mL
4 tbsp vinegar	60 mL
2 cups light cream	500 mL

Sauté lobster in butter for 5 minutes. Add vinegar and continue cooking. Add cream and bring back to serving temperature. Serves 4.

Baked Halibut in Cream
Compass Rose

4 halibut steaks, individual serving size	4
1 chicken bouillon cube, crumbled	1
1/4 tsp pepper	1 mL
1/2 tsp lemon juice	2 mL
1/4 cup parsley, chopped	50 mL
1/2 cup Cheddar cheese, grated	125 mL
3/4 cup heavy cream	175 mL

Place halibut steaks in a greased baking dish. Sprinkle with bouillon, pepper, lemon juice, parsley and cheese. Pour cream over fish. Bake at 500°F (250°C) until cream bubbles, approximately 10 minutes. Reduce heat to 325°F (160°C) and continue to bake until tender, 8 to 10 minutes. Serve on a lettuce or spinach leaf garnished with cucumber and lemon slices. Serves 4.

Scallops à Ma Façon
L' Auberge

1 1/2 lb scallops	750 g
3 tbsp butter	45 mL
Pinch of salt and pepper	Pinch
2 tbsp garlic butter	30 mL
Splash of Pernod liqueur	Splash

Cut scallops in two. Sauté in butter in a heavy skillet. Season with salt and pepper. When lightly browned, add garlic butter (cream butter; when it is very soft, add one garlic clove that has been puréed). Bring to a very high heat and splash with Pernod. Ignite and serve on a bed of fettuccine. Serves 4.

Fillet of Sole with Mussels
Upper Deck Restaurant

1 1/2 lb sole	750 g
2 green onions, chopped	2
24 mussels	24
4 tbsp butter	60 mL
1/3 cup lemon juice	75 mL
2 tbsp parsley, chopped	30 mL
Salt and pepper to taste	

Gently poach the sole in a fish stock to which the chopped green onions have been added. Drain and set on a warm platter. Steam the mussels, remove from shells and take off beards. Place mussels around the sole. Brush with hot butter, lemon juice and chopped parsley. Season to taste. Serves 4.

The Manor Inn Scallop Provençale
The Manor Inn

1 lb medium scallops	500 g
1-2 tbsp butter	15-30 mL
Dash of garlic powder	Dash
1/2 tsp lemon juice	2 mL
2 cups mushrooms, sliced	250 mL
1/4 cup white wine	50 mL
1 tomato, diced	1

Sauté scallops in butter, add garlic powder, lemon juice and mushrooms. Simmer for a few minutes, then add the wine and tomato. Stir over low heat until it makes its own sauce.

Serve in traditional scallop shell and garnish with lemon wedge and a sprig of parsley. Serves 3 to 4.

Halibut in Cider
Bayberry House

1/4 cup onion, chopped	50 mL
1/2 cup mushrooms, chopped	125 mL
2 tbsp butter	30 mL
4 halibut steaks, individual serving size	4
Salt and pepper to taste	
1 cup hard cider	250 mL
2 egg yolks	2
3/4 cup heavy cream	175 mL
Parsley, chopped	

Lightly sweat the onion and mushrooms in butter. Add the halibut steaks and turn once so they are coated with butter. Season with salt and pepper. Add the cider and cover the pan with waxed paper. Place in a 350°F (180°C) oven and poach for 15 to 20 minutes. Remove fish to a serving platter and keep warm.

Place the poaching liquid over fairly high heat and reduce by half. Whisk the egg yolks and cream together and add to remaining cider. Whisk over a gentle heat until slightly thickened. Spoon over fish. Sprinkle with chopped parsley. Serves 4.

EGGS
AND
CHEESE

Vegetable Cheesecake
Blue Heron Inn

3-4 tbsp bread crumbs	45-60 mL
3 cups zucchini, grated	750 mL
1 tsp salt	5 mL
1 cup onion, minced	250 mL
3 tbsp butter	45 mL
1/2 tsp salt	2 mL
1 cup carrot, grated	250 mL
2-3 garlic cloves, crushed	2-3
3 tbsp flour	45 mL
1/2 tsp each of basil and oregano	2 mL
1/4 cup fresh parsley, minced	50 mL
1 tbsp lemon juice	15 mL
3 cups ricotta or cottage cheese	750 mL
1 cup mozzarella cheese, grated	250 mL
1/2 cup Parmesan cheese, grated	125 mL
4 eggs at room temperature	4
Salt and pepper to taste	
Tomatoes, sliced (optional)	

Butter a 10-inch (25-cm) springform pan and sprinkle in bread crumbs.

Set zucchini in a colander and add 1 tsp salt. Let stand 15 minutes; squeeze out moisture.

In a large skillet, sauté onion in butter and 1/2 tsp (2 mL) salt. After several minutes, add carrot, zucchini, garlic, flour, basil and oregano. Keep stirring over medium heat for 8 to 10 minutes. Remove from heat and stir in parsley and lemon juice.

With an electric mixer, beat together at high speed the cheeses and eggs, until well blended. Add sautéed vegetables and mix well. Season to taste with salt and pepper.

Turn mixture into a prepared pan. Bake, uncovered, at 375 degrees F (190°C) for 1/2 hour. Reduce oven heat to 350°F (180°C) and decorate top with thin slices of tomatoes, if desired. Continue to bake for an additional 1/2 hour. Turn off oven, open door and let cake stand 15 minutes longer. Remove from oven and let cool 10 minutes before serving. Serves 6 to 8.

Quiche Lorraine
Gowrie

2/3 cup butter	150 mL
1 1/2 cups flour	375 mL
1/4 tsp salt	1 mL
2 egg yolks	2

Filling:

10 slices bacon, crisply cooked	10
1 1/2 cups Gruyère cheese, cut in small cubes	375 mL
4 eggs, beaten	4
1 3/4 cups light cream	450 mL
Nutmeg, grated	

Blend butter, flour and salt together with a pastry blender. Beat the egg yolks and blend into the dough until it holds together. Shape into a ball and chill for 1/2 hour. On a floured board, roll into a circle to fit a 10-inch (1.5-L) quiche pan.

Scatter bacon and cheese in bottom of quiche shell. Beat the eggs with light cream and pour into pastry. Grate nutmeg on top. Place on lowest rack in oven and bake at 350°F (180°C) for 50 minutes, until filling is puffed and lightly browned. Let stand 15 minutes before cutting.

Normaway-style French Toast
The Normaway Inn

5 eggs	5
1/4 cup milk	50 mL
1 cup rolled oats	250 mL
1/4 cup white sugar	50 mL
1/2 tsp cinnamon	2 mL
6-8 bread slices	6-8

Beat eggs and milk. In a separate bowl combine oats, sugar and cinnamon. Dip bread slices in egg and then dredge in dry mixture.

Fry bread on both sides in a greased pan. Serve with maple syrup.

VEGETABLES

Ratatouille Niçoise
Garrison House Inn

3 cups onions, chopped	750 mL
1/2 cup olive oil	125 mL
6 tomatoes, cut in 1/2-inch cubes	6
4 medium zucchini, cut in 1/2-inch cubes	4
1 medium eggplant, cut in 1/2-inch cubes	1
2 red peppers, cut in 1/2-inch squares	2
2 large garlic cloves, crushed	2
2 cups cheese of choice, grated	500 mL
1 cup fine bread crumbs	250 mL

Sweat onions in olive oil over low heat until soft. Add tomatoes and cook for 3 to 4 minutes. Add the rest of the ingredients, except cheese and bread crumbs, and cook over low heat for 1 hour. Uncover and continue cooking to reduce, until liquid is desired consistency.

Combine cheese and bread crumbs and sprinkle over vegetables. Place under broiler until cheese has melted. Serves 4 to 6.

Baked Beans with Molasses
The Bright House

1 lb yellow-eyed beans	500 g
1/4 lb salt pork, diced	125 g
1 cup onion, finely chopped	250 mL
1/4 cup brown sugar	50 mL
1/2 cup molasses	125 mL
1/2 tsp salt	2 mL
1 tbsp dry mustard	15 mL

Wash beans well, pick over any blemished beans and soak overnight. Simmer approximately 1 hour, until beans are just tender. Skim as necessary.

Place beans, with enough cooking water to cover about 1 inch (5 cm), in a large earthenware casserole with a tight lid. Mix the remaining ingredients and add to the casserole.

Bake, covered, at 200°F (100°C) for 8 hours. Shake occasionally and add more water if necessary. Uncover pot for last hour to brown top. Serves 4 to 6.

Red Cabbage
The Normaway Inn

1/2 red cabbage, about 1 lb	about 500 g
2 tbsp onion, chopped	30 mL
1 1/2 tbsp butter	25 mL
1 apple	1
1/4 tsp salt	1 mL
2 tbsp vinegar	30 mL
2 tbsp brown sugar	30 mL

Shred cabbage and soak in cold water. Sauté the onion in butter. When soft, add the drained, yet moist, cabbage and simmer, covered, for 10 minutes. Core and thinly slice the apple. Add apple, salt, vinegar and sugar to cabbage.

Simmer slowly for 1 1/2 hours. Add boiling water during cooking if necessary. If the water has not been absorbed during cooking, remove the cover and cook gently until it is reduced.

Baked Squash and Pearl Onions
Blomidon Inn

1 cup pearl onions	250 mL
1/4 cup butter	50 mL
1/2 cup cabbage, finely shredded	125 mL
3 cups dry squash, cooked and mashed	750 mL
2/3 cup sour cream	150 mL
Fresh dill and/or fresh parsley to taste	
Pepper to taste	

Blanch onions for 1 minute and then sauté in half the butter until barely tender. Steam shredded cabbage until tender.

Combine squash, cabbage, onions, sour cream and seasonings in a greased casserole. Dot with remaining butter and bake in a 350°F (180°C) oven for 1/2 hour, until brown. Serves 6 to 8.

Potatoes Dauphinois
Compass Rose

6-8 medium potatoes, pared and sliced thinly	6-8
Garlic salt and pepper to taste	
4 tbsp butter	60 mL
3/4 cup light cream	175 mL
3/4 cup heavy cream	175 mL

Place one-third of the potatoes in a greased casserole. Sprinkle with garlic salt and pepper. Repeat with 2 more layers. Dot butter on top of potatoes. Combine light and heavy cream and pour over potatoes. Preheat oven to 375°F (190°C) and bake until brown and bubbly, about 1 hour.

Mushroom Cream Sauce
Blue Heron Inn

1/2 cup scallions, chopped	125 mL
3/4 cup butter	175 mL
3 cups fresh mushrooms, sliced	750 mL
5 tbsp flour	75 mL
2 cups milk	500 mL
1 1/2 cups mozzarella cheese, grated	375 mL
1/2 cup Parmesan cheese	125 mL
Salt and pepper to taste	

Sauté scallions in butter for several minutes. Add mushrooms and sauté an additional 5 to 10 minutes.

Add flour and milk, a little at a time, alternating the two and stirring constantly until sauce is smooth. Add cheeses and stir. Add salt and pepper to taste. Serve over hot vermicelli or other pasta. Garnish with fresh parsley. Serves 4.

German-style Potato Salad
Compass Rose

6 medium-sized potatoes	6
Sprinkle of each of parsley, pepper, garlic salt, lemon juice and Worcestershire sauce	Sprinkle
Italian salad dressing	

Wash, but do not peel, the potatoes. Cut into small cubes. Steam until fork-tender, about 10 minutes.

Mix warm potatoes with parsley, pepper, garlic salt, lemon juice, Worcestershire sauce and a sufficient amount of commercial Italian salad dressing to glaze the potatoes nicely. Serve warm or chilled. Serves 4 to 6.

Curried Rice Pilaf
The Pines Resort Hotel

1 small onion, finely chopped	1
2 tbsp oil	30 mL
Pinch of curry powder	Pinch
1 1/4 cup long-grain rice	300 mL
1 bay leaf	1
Salt and pepper to taste	
2 1/2 cups light chicken stock	625 mL

Sweat the chopped onion in oil for 2 minutes. Add curry powder, rice, bay leaf, salt and pepper. Mix well. Add the chicken stock, cover and cook over low to medium heat for 12 minutes. Remove from heat and let stand, covered, for 10 minutes. Remove bay leaf and serve. Serves 4 to 6.

Polynesian Baked Tomatoes
Clipper Cay

1/2 cup dry bread crumbs	125 mL
1/4 tsp basil	1 mL
1 hard-boiled egg, diced	1
Salt and pepper to taste	
4 large, ripe tomatoes, halved	4
5 tbsp butter	75 mL

Mix bread crumbs, basil and egg together. Add salt and pepper to taste. Top each tomato with mixture and dot with butter. Bake at 325°F (160°C) for 8 to 10 minutes. Brown under broiler.

Turnip and Apple Bake
Blomidon Inn

2 apples	2
1 tsp sugar	5 mL
3 cups turnip, cooked and mashed	750 mL
1/2 cup heavy cream	125 mL
2 tbsp butter	30 mL

Core and slice apples. Poach in water with sugar until barely soft. Layer turnip and apple in a baking dish. Top with cream and dot with butter. Bake at 350°F (180°C) for 1/2 hour.

PIES, CAKES
AND
COOKIES

Chocolate Cake
Harris' Seafood Restaurant

1 cup butter	250 mL
2 cups plus 2 tbsp white sugar	530 mL
4 eggs, beaten	4
2 1/2 cups flour	625 mL
2 tsp baking soda	10 mL
1/2 tsp salt	2 mL
3/4 cups cocoa	175 mL
1 cup sour milk	250 mL
1 cup hot water	250 mL
1 tsp vanilla	5 mL

White Mountain Frosting:	
3 egg whites	3
2 cups white sugar	500 mL
4 tbsp water	60 mL
1 tbsp corn syrup	15 mL
Pinch of salt	Pinch
1 tsp vanilla	5 mL

Cream butter and sugar until light and fluffy. Add 4 beaten eggs. Sift flour, baking soda, salt and cocoa together and add to butter mixture, alternating with the sour milk. Add the hot water and vanilla.

Grease and flour two 9-inch (1.5-L) cake pans. Divide mixture between pans and bake at 350°F (180°C) for 3/4 hour or until a toothpick inserted in the centre of the cake comes out clean. Cool on racks. Cover with White Mountain Frosting.

To prepare frosting, put all frosting ingredients, except vanilla, in a double boiler and beat, over boiling water, with a hand-mixer or rotary beater until double in bulk, about 7 minutes. Add vanilla, remove from stove and continue to beat for a few minutes.

Cranberry Squares
The Mug Up

2 cups rolled oats	500 mL
1 cup flour	250 mL
1 cup brown sugar	250 mL
1 tsp baking soda	5 mL
3/4 cup butter	175 mL
1 1/4 cups cranberry sauce	300 mL

Mix rolled oats, flour, brown sugar and baking soda in a bowl. Melt butter and add to dry mixture, mixing well. Place half of the mixture in a greased 9-inch (2.5-L) square pan. Cover with the cranberries and top with the remaining half of the mixture. Press lightly. Bake at 350°F (180°C) for approximately 1/2 hour.

Rangers
Milford House

1/2 cup butter	125 mL
1/2 cup white sugar	125 mL
1/2 cup brown sugar	125 mL
1 egg, slightly beaten	1
1 tsp vanilla	5 mL
1 cup flour	250 mL
1/2 tsp baking soda	2 mL
1/2 tsp baking powder	2 mL
1/4 tsp salt	1 mL
1 cup Rice Krispies	250 mL
1 cup rolled oats	250 mL
1/2 cup raisins	125 mL

Cream butter and sugars. Add slightly beaten egg and vanilla and beat. Add flour, baking soda, baking powder and salt to mixture and combine well. Mix in the Rice Krispies, rolled oats and raisins.

Drop by teaspoons on a greased baking sheet and bake in a 350°F (180°C) oven for 10 minutes or until golden brown.

Buttermilk Pie
Gramma's House

4 eggs	4
1/4 cup flour	50 mL
1 cup white sugar	250 mL
1/2 tsp salt	2 mL
2 cups buttermilk	500 mL
Pastry (recipe follows)	

Beat eggs, add flour, a little at a time, and continue to beat. Add sugar and salt; mix well. Add buttermilk and pour into an unbaked pie shell. Bake 40 to 45 minutes at 375°F (190°C).

Pastry — supplied by authors:	
1 cup flour	250 mL
1/4 tsp salt	1 mL
1/2 cup shortening	125 mL
2-3 tbsp cold water	30-45 mL

Combine flour and salt in mixing bowl. Cut shortening into flour with pastry blender or 2 forks until mixture is size of large peas. Do not overmix. Sprinkle cold water over mixture and blend with a fork until absorbed. Form into a ball and roll out on a floured surface. Yields enough pastry for a single shell.

Molasses Cookies
The Mug Up

2 cups molasses	500 mL
1 cup lard	250 mL
1/2 tsp cloves	2 mL
1 tsp nutmeg	5 mL
2 tsp ginger	10 mL
2 tsp cinnamon	10 mL
2 tsp baking soda	10 mL
1 egg, beaten	1
5 cups flour	1.25 L

Bring molasses, lard, cloves, nutmeg, ginger, cinnamon and baking soda to a boil. Cool and add the beaten egg. Mix in the flour and roll in balls. Place on a greased cookie sheet and press with a fork. Bake at 350°F (180°C) for 12 minutes. Yields 24 large cookies.

Pumpkin Pie
Harris' Seafood Restaurant

3 eggs, beaten	3
1 1/2 cups cooked pumpkin	375 mL
1/2 cup white sugar	125 mL
1/2 cup brown sugar	125 mL
1/2 tsp salt	2 mL
1/2 tsp vanilla	2 mL
1 tsp ginger	5 mL
1/2 tsp cinnamon	2 mL
1 cup whole milk	250 mL
1 cup evaporated milk	250 mL
Unbaked pie shell	

Beat eggs. Add pumpkin, sugars, salt and vanilla. Stir in the spices, the whole milk and the evaporated milk. Pour into an unbaked pie shell in a 9-inch (1-L) pie plate. Bake at 350°F (180°C) until centre is firm, about 1 hour.

Coffee Ice Cream Pie
Highland Heights Inn

2 1-oz. squares unsweetened chocolate	60 g
1 tbsp butter	15 mL
2 tbsp hot milk	30 mL
2/3 cup sifted confectioner's sugar	150 mL
1 1/2 cups shredded coconut	375 mL
1 qt vanilla ice cream	1 L
2 tsp instant coffee	10 mL
1/4 cup chopped nuts	50 mL

Melt chocolate and butter over hot water and blend. Stir milk into confectioner's sugar, then add to the chocolate mixture. Mix well. Stir in coconut. Press into bottom and sides of a buttered 9-inch (1-L) pie plate. Chill in the refrigerator.

Stir ice cream until softened. Mix in instant coffee and place in pie shell. Sprinkle nuts on top. Freeze and serve.

BREADS
AND
MUFFINS

Scottish Oatcakes
Inverary Inn

3 cups rolled oats	750 mL
2 cups flour	500 mL
1 cup brown sugar	250 mL
1/2 tsp salt	2 mL
1/2 lb lard	250 g
1/2 tsp baking soda	2 mL
1/2 cup hot water	125 mL

Combine dry ingredients, except baking soda. Work in the lard with fingers. Add baking soda to hot water, then add to mixture, a little at a time, until dough is ready to roll. Roll out on floured surface and cut in squares. Place on a greased cookie sheet.

Bake at 400°F (200°C) for 10 to 12 minutes.

Orange and Raisin Muffins
The Zwicker Inn

3/4 cup raisins	175 mL
1 1/4 cups all-purpose flour	300 mL
1/2 cup whole wheat flour	125 mL
1/4 cup sugar	50 mL
1 tbsp baking powder	15 mL
1/2 tsp salt	2 mL
1 egg	1
1/3 cup butter, melted	75 mL
1/2 cup milk	125 mL
1/4 cup orange juice	50 mL

Soak raisins in hot water for 5 minutes. Drain, dry on paper towels and toss with flour to coat.

Combine dry ingredients and mix well. In another bowl beat egg and continue to beat while adding melted butter, milk and orange juice. Combine wet and dry ingredients, until barely mixed.

Bake in 400°F (200°C) oven for 12 to 15 minutes, until done. Yields 8 to 10 large muffins.

Molasses Whole Wheat Bread
The Bright House

2 tbsp dry yeast	30 mL
3/4 cup lukewarm water	175 mL
1 tsp sugar	5 mL
2 cups hot water	500 mL
1 cup molasses	250 mL
2 tbsp vegetable oil	30 mL
2 tsp salt	10 mL
3 cups white flour	750 mL
5 cups whole wheat flour	1.25 L

Dissolve yeast in lukewarm water with sugar. Let stand for 10 minutes. To hot water, add molasses, oil and salt. Beat mixture and cool. Add yeast mixture and white flour. Beat well. Gradually add the whole wheat flour. Knead for 12 minutes, until smooth and elastic.

Place dough in a greased bowl and turn to grease the top. Cover with plastic wrap and let rise until double. Punch down and knead for 2 minutes, shape into bread or rolls and place in well-greased pans. Let rise until double.

Bake at 350°F (180°C) for about 40 minutes, until well browned and hollow-sounding when tapped. Yields 4 loaves.

Vina Percy's Bran Muffins
The Moorings

1 cup bran	250 mL
1 cup dates or raisins	250 mL
1 cup boiling water	250 mL
2 eggs	2
1/2 cup white sugar	125 mL
1/4 cup molasses	50 mL
1/2 cup oil	125 mL
2 cups buttermilk	500 mL
2 1/2 cups flour	625 mL
1 1/2 tbsp baking soda	25 mL
1/2 tsp salt	2 mL
2 cups bran flakes	500 mL

Mix bran, dates or raisins, and boiling water. Let stand until cold. Combine eggs, sugar, molasses, oil and buttermilk; add to bran mixture and beat.

Sift together flour, baking soda and salt. Add to above mixture. Stir in bran flakes. Bake at 375°F (190°C) for approximately 20 minutes.

Yields 24 muffins. Batter may be refrigerated for several days to use as needed.

Bonnach
Inverary Inn

4 cups flour	1 L
8 tsp baking powder	40 mL
2 tsp salt	10 mL
1/2 cup white sugar	125 mL
1/2 cup shortening	125 mL
1/2 cup currants	125 mL
1 1/2 cups milk	375 mL

Combine flour, baking powder, salt and sugar. Work in shortening as for pastry. Add currants. Moisten with milk, making a soft dough. Knead 10 seconds. Pat out on a greased cookie sheet, to a thickness of 1/2 inch (1 cm). Preheat oven to 375°F (190°C) and bake for 25 minutes. Serve warm with butter.

Brown Bread
Inverary Inn

2 tbsp dry yeast	30 mL
1 cup lukewarm water	250 mL
3 cups hot water	750 mL
1 tbsp salt	15 mL
3 tbsp shortening	45 mL
1 cup molasses	250 mL
2 cups rolled oats	500 mL
8 cups flour	2 L

Soften dry yeast in lukewarm water. Let stand 10 minutes. In a separate bowl place hot water, salt, shortening, molasses and rolled oats. Beat mixture and cool. Stir in the yeast mixture. Slowly add flour, a little at a time. Turn out on a floured board and knead 7 to 10 minutes. Place in a greased bowl and turn to grease top. Cover and let rise 1 hour. Knead again and place in greased bread pans. Let rise 1 hour. Bake at 350°F (175°C) for 1 hour. Yields 2 double loaves.

White Bread
Compass Rose

2 tbsp yeast	30 mL
1 tbsp sugar	15 mL
1/2 cup lukewarm water	125 mL
4 cups milk, slightly heated	1 L
4 tbsp lard	60 mL
4 tbsp sugar or honey	60 mL
1 tbsp salt	15 mL
1 tsp garlic salt	5 mL
10 cups flour	2.5 L
1 egg yolk	1
Poppy seeds (optional)	

Dissolve yeast and 1 tbsp (15 mL) sugar in lukewarm water. Set aside for 10 minutes.

Combine milk, lard, 4 tbsp (60 mL) sugar or honey, salt and garlic salt. Cool slightly. Add 8 cups of flour (2 L), a little at a time, mixing thoroughly. Mix in yeast mixture. Gradually add the additional flour. Remove from the bowl and knead on a floured board for 7 minutes.

Place dough in a greased bowl and turn to cover ball with oil. Cover and let rise for 1 hour in a warm, draft-free place.

Punch down and shape into 3 double loaves. Place in greased pans and glaze with an egg yolk. Sprinkle with poppy seeds, if desired. Let rise for 1 hour. Bake in a preheated 350°F (180°C) oven for 35 minutes or until loaves are golden brown and sound hollow when tapped on the bottom.

Herb Bread
The Bright House

1 tbsp dry yeast	15 mL
1/2 cup lukewarm water	125 mL
1 tsp sugar	5 mL
1 1/2 cups lukewarm water	375 mL
1 tbsp salt	15 mL
1 1/2 tbsp mixed dried herbs	25 mL
1 tbsp lemon juice	15 mL
1/2 tsp lemon zest, finely grated	2 mL
5-6 cups white flour	1.25-1.5 L
1 egg white, lightly beaten	1

Dissolve yeast in 1/2 cup (125 mL) lukewarm water with sugar for 10 minutes. In a large bowl add 1 1/2 cups (375 mL) lukewarm water, salt, herbs, lemon juice, zest, yeast mixture and 3 cups of the flour. Beat well.

Gradually add remaining flour until it forms a very firm dough. Knead well for 10 minutes, until smooth and elastic. Put ball of dough in a well-oiled bowl and roll it around until well coated. Cover bowl with a clean cloth and let rise until doubled in bulk. Punch down and knead for 2 minutes.

Divide dough into 2 portions. Roll out each portion into a large rectangle about 2 inches shorter than the length of the baking sheet. Roll up lengthwise as tightly as possible. Place seam-side down on a well-greased baking sheet and taper the ends. Cut diagonal slashes along the top of each loaf. Let rise again until double. Brush tops with lightly beaten egg white. Bake in preheated 400°F (200°C) oven for 20 minutes, until golden and hollow-sounding.

DESSERTS

Classic English Trifle
Garrison House Inn

8 ladyfingers or 1 sponge cake	8 or 1
1/2 cup jam of choice	125 mL
1/4 cup sherry	50 mL
1 1/2 cups seasonal fruit and juice	375 mL
Custard (recipe follows)	
1/2 cup heavy cream	125 mL
1/2 tsp vanilla	2 mL
1/4 cup almonds, sliced	50 mL

Split ladyfingers or cake and spread with thick layer of jam. Arrange pieces over the bottom of a shallow, clear glass bowl. Sprinkle sherry over cake. Arrange fruit and juice on cake. Prepare custard and while still warm pour over trifle. Let stand at room temperature until cool and then refrigerate.

To serve, whip cream until stiff and add vanilla. Spread over custard and top with almonds and extra fruit. Serves 6 to 8.

Egg Custard — supplied by authors:

1/4 cup sugar	50 mL
3 tbsp flour	45 mL
3 egg yolks, beaten	3
2 cups milk	500 mL
2 tsp lemon zest	10 mL
1 tsp vanilla	5 mL

In a heavy saucepan combine sugar, flour, egg yolks, milk and lemon zest. Cook and stir over medium heat until mixture is thick and begins to boil. Remove from heat, add vanilla and cover with waxed paper.

Apple Crêpe Supreme
Dublin Bay House

1/2 cup dark brown sugar	125 mL
2 tbsp water	30 mL
1/3 cup currants	75 mL
3 tbsp lemon juice	45 mL
1 1/2 tsp cinnamon	7 mL
1 1/2 lb firm cooking apples	750 g
1 1/2 tsp cornstarch dissolved in 2 tbsp water	7 mL and 30 mL
6 thin crêpes (recipe follows)	6
1/2 cup heavy cream, whipped	125 mL

Combine sugar, water, currants, lemon juice and cinnamon. Simmer until currants are plump. Peel and cut apples into thin slices. Add apples to currant mixture and simmer 15 minutes, until apples are slightly softened. Stir in cornstarch and water and let cook only until sauce is slightly thickened.

Spread sauce on crêpes, roll and top with another spoon of sauce and whipped cream. Serves 4 to 6. (Leftover apple is equally good on pancakes, ice cream and waffles.)

Crêpes — supplied by authors:	
3/4 cup flour	175 mL
1/2 tsp salt	2 mL
1 tsp baking powder	5 mL
2 tbsp powdered sugar (optional)	30 mL
2 eggs	2
2/3 cup milk	150 mL
1/3 cup water	75 mL
1/2 tsp vanilla	2 mL

Sift flour and resift with other dry ingredients. In a separate bowl beat eggs. Add milk, water and vanilla and beat. Make a well in dry ingredients. Pour in liquid and combine with a few swift strokes. Ignore the lumps.

Lightly oil a skillet over moderate heat. Add a small amount of the batter and tip the skillet to spread. When lightly browned, flip crêpe and brown the other side. Makes 14 to 16 crêpes. May be frozen.

Frozen Cappuccino
Boscawen Inn

1/2 cup sugar	125 mL
1/2 cup water	125 mL
2 tsp instant coffee	10 mL
1 cup semisweet chocolate chips	250 mL
2 eggs	2
1/2 tsp cinnamon	2 mL
1 1/2 cups heavy cream	375 mL

Combine sugar, water and coffee and boil for 3 minutes. Cool. Put chocolate chips in a blender or food processor and add eggs, cinnamon and coffee syrup. Blend for 2 minutes. Whip cream and fold into chocolate syrup. Portion in serving dishes and freeze overnight. Serves 6.

Spumoni Mocha
Bayberry House

1/3 cup coffee liqueur	75 mL
3 egg yolks	3
3 tbsp sugar	45 mL
2 tsp water	10 mL
1/4 tsp almond extract	1 mL
3/4 cups heavy cream, whipped	175 mL

Put the liqueur, egg yolks, sugar, water and almond extract in a heatproof bowl over boiling water. Immediately turn the water to a bare simmer. Beat the ingredients with a wire whisk until the mixture is warm and begins to thicken. Do not allow the water to boil.

Remove from over the water and whip the ingredients until smooth and thick. Fold in the whipped cream and mix carefully; cool. Spoon into custard cups, cover with waxed paper and place in the freezer for 6 hours. Serves 4 to 6.

Crème Caramel
Gowrie

Caramel:	
1/3 cup sugar	75 mL
2 tbsp boiling water	30 mL

Custard:	
3 cups milk	750 mL
4 egg yolks	4
1 whole egg	1
Pinch of salt	Pinch
1/4 cup sugar	50 mL
2 tbsp sherry or 2 tsp vanilla	30 mL or 10 mL

To prepare the caramel, in a heavy saucepan over high heat melt sugar until golden, being careful it does not scorch. Slowly, while stirring carefully, add boiling water. Immediately turn into a 1-qt (1-L) casserole or individual ramekins, to cover bottom.

To prepare the custard, heat milk to scalding. In a large bowl whip egg yolks, whole egg, salt and sugar. Slowly pour heated milk into egg mixture, stirring constantly. Add sherry or vanilla, as desired. Skim foam off custard and strain into caramel-covered casserole. Place in a water bath in a 325°F (160°C) oven until barely set, 1 hour or more. Chill. To serve, run a knife around the edge of custard and invert on a rimmed serving dish. Serves 6.

Raspberry Flan
Blue Heron Inn

1 cup flour	250 mL
Pinch of salt	Pinch
2 tbsp sugar	30 mL
1/2 cup butter	125 mL
1 tbsp vinegar	15 mL
1 cup sugar	250 mL
2 tbsp flour	30 mL
3 cups raspberries, fresh or frozen	750 mL

Combine 1 cup (250 mL) flour, salt and 2 tbsp (30 mL) sugar. Add butter and vinegar and mix well. Press gently into a 9-inch (1-L) pie plate.

Gently mix together 1 cup (250 mL) sugar, 2 tbsp (30 mL) flour and 2 cups (500 mL) of the raspberries. Pour over crust and bake at 400°F (200°C) for 50 to 60 minutes. Sprinkle with remaining berries, chill and serve. (Experiment with other berries if you wish.)

Cheesecake Tart

The Bright House

Unbaked pastry shell	
2/3 cup cottage cheese, creamed	150 mL
1/2 cup sour cream	125 mL
1/2 cup milk	125 mL
1 tbsp lemon juice	15 mL
Grated peel of 1/2 lemon	
1/4 tsp mace	1 mL
1/2 tsp vanilla	2 mL
2 tbsp cornstarch	30 mL
1 tbsp butter, melted	15 mL
2 eggs, separated	2
1/2 cup sugar	125 mL
Pinch of salt	Pinch
Strawberry Sauce:	
1 cup water	250 mL
1 tbsp cornstarch	15 mL
1/2 cup sugar	125 mL
1 tbsp butter	15 mL
Dash of salt	Dash
10 oz frozen strawberries	300 g

Line a deep, 10-inch (1.2-L) pie plate with pastry of your choice.

Blend together all tart ingredients, except egg whites, 2 tbsp (30 mL) sugar and a pinch of salt, until smooth and creamy. Beat egg whites until stiff, adding 2 tbsp (30 mL) sugar and salt.

Fold mixture together very gently and pour into shell. Bake at 400°F (200°C) for 10 minutes, then at 350 degrees F (180°C) for 25 minutes or until set. Serve with Strawberry Sauce.

To prepare sauce, combine water, cornstarch, sugar, butter and salt with a wire whisk. Bring to a boil and cook 5 minutes, whisking constantly. Add frozen strawberries and stir until berries are defrosted. Cool and refrigerate.

Carrot Pudding
Upper Deck Restaurant

1/2 tsp baking soda	2 mL
1/2 cup potato, grated	125 mL
1/2 cup all-purpose flour	125 mL
1/2 cup raisins	125 mL
1/2 cup brown sugar	125 mL
1/2 cup beef suet	125 mL
2 tbsp lemon juice	30 mL
1/2 tsp lemon zest	2 mL
1/2 tsp cloves	2 mL
1/2 tsp cinnamon	2 mL
1/2 cup carrot, grated	125 mL
1/2 tsp salt	2 mL

With a brush, butter the inside of a 4-cup (1-L) mold. Mix the baking soda with the potato, then combine with all remaining ingredients. Put the mixture into the mold. Cover with foil and place the mold in a water bath. Bake at 350°F (180°C) for 2 hours and 40 minutes. Serves 4 to 6.

Serve warm with topping of your choice (whipped cream, hard sauce, lemon sauce, etc.).

Stuffed Baked Apples
Clipper Cay

6 large cooking apples	6
1 cup cake or vanilla cookie crumbs	250 mL
1/3 cup raisins	75 mL
1/4 tsp cinnamon	1 mL
1/4 cup maple syrup	50 mL
12 strips puff pastry, 1/2 inch x 8 inches (1 cm x 20 cm)	12
1 egg	1
1 tsp water	5 mL

Maple Cream Sauce:	
1/4 cup sugar	50 mL
1 1/2 tbsp flour	25 mL
Pinch of salt	Pinch
1/2 cup milk	125 mL
2 egg yolks, beaten	2
2 tbsp butter	30 mL
1/4 tsp vanilla	1 mL
Dark rum to taste (optional)	
1/4 cup maple syrup	50 mL

Peel and core apples. Combine crumbs, raisins, cinnamon and maple syrup and add to apple cavities. Wrap pastry around each apple, forming a cage. Pinch top of dough. Place in a baking dish and brush with an egg wash (egg and water, beaten). Bake at 350°F (180°C) for 50 minutes. Serve warm with Maple Cream Sauce.

To prepare sauce, combine sugar, flour and salt in a saucepan. Gradually stir in milk. Cook and stir over medium heat until mixture comes to a boil. Remove from heat.

Stir a small amount of the hot mixture into beaten egg yolks. Return to the hot mixture and cook 2 minutes, stirring constantly. Remove from heat, add butter, vanilla and rum, if desired. Cover with waxed paper and cool.

Divide sauce among 6 serving dishes. Pour maple syrup over cream and add warm apples.

Blueberry Sour Cream Cake
The Cape House Inn

Crust:

1 1/2 cups flour	375 mL
1/2 cup sugar	125 mL
1 1/2 tsp baking powder	7 mL
1/2 cup butter	125 mL
1 egg	1
1 tsp vanilla	5 mL

Filling:

4 cups fresh or frozen blueberries	1 L
2 cups sour cream	500 mL
1/3 cup sugar	75 mL
2 egg yolks	2
1 tsp vanilla	5 mL
Whipped cream (optional)	

To prepare crust, blend flour, sugar, baking powder and butter in a mixing bowl. Add egg and vanilla and blend. Pat dough over the base of a 9-inch (23-cm) springform pan.

Top crust with 3 cups (750 mL) of the blueberries. Mix sour cream, sugar, egg yolks and vanilla together and pour over berries. Bake for 1 hour in a 375°F (190°C) oven, until edges of cream mixture are lightly browned. Garnish with remaining berries and whipped cream, if desired. Serves 8 to 10.

Swiss Chocolate Truffle Cake
Keltic Lodge

1 3/4 cups heavy cream	450 mL
2 slices of chocolate sponge cake, 1/2 inch x 8 inches (1.25 cm x 20 cm); any instant mix will suffice	2

Ganache:

14 oz. semisweet chocolate	400 g
1/3 cup heavy cream	75 mL
4 tbsp dark rum	60 mL
1/2 tsp butter	2 mL

Syrup:

2 tbsp sugar	30 mL
2 tbsp water	30 mL
2 tbsp rum	30 mL

To prepare the syrup, place sugar and water in a small saucepan, bring to a boil and remove from heat. Pour into a cup for cooling, stir in rum and cover with plastic wrap.

To prepare the ganache, melt the chocolate, along with the other ganache ingredients, over a double boiler. Do not let the water in the pot come to a boil.

While the chocolate is melting, whip the 1 3/4 cups (450 mL) cream and place in the refrigerator. Be sure the bowl, beaters and cream are well chilled before whipping.

With a whisk, stir the chocolate well, until smooth. Return to the double boiler to keep warm, 100 to 110°F (35 to 40°C). Place a slice of cake in an 8-inch (20-cm) springform pan that is lined with waxed paper and brush cake with half of the syrup.

Quickly and gently fold the ganache into the cream. Pour half of the cream into the pan. Place the second layer of cake on top, press down gently and brush with remaining syrup. Fill in the rest of the ganache, spread and smooth off the top.

Chill overnight in the refrigerator. Remove from the springform pan, decorate if desired and serve.

Hazelnut Cheesecake
Inn Bear River

1/2 lb cream cheese	250 g
1/3 cup yogurt	75 mL
1/3 cup sugar	75 mL
2 tsp flour	10 mL
2 tbsp lemon juice	30 mL
3/4 tsp vanilla	4 mL
2 egg yolks	2
2 tbsp hazelnuts, ground	30 mL
2 egg whites, room temperature	2
Graham cracker crust	

Beat cream cheese and yogurt until smooth. Beat in sugar and flour. Add lemon juice and vanilla. Beat in egg yolks, one at a time. Stir in the ground nuts.

Beat egg whites until stiff. Fold into the cheese mixture. Turn into an 8-inch (20-cm) springform pan that is lined with a graham cracker crust. Bake at 275°F (135°C) for 1 hour and 15 minutes. Chill at least 6 hours. (The chef says that he always puts a fruit topping on the inn's cheesecake, but that it stands well on its own.)

Blueberry Topping — supplied by authors:

1 1/2 cups blueberries	375 mL
1/2 cup sugar	125 mL
1/2 cup light corn syrup	125 mL
1/2 tsp lemon juice	2 mL

Combine ingredients in a heavy-bottomed saucepan and place over medium heat. Stir constantly until sugar is dissolved. Bring to a boil and cook 3 to 5 minutes. Cool slightly and pour on cake top.

Amaretto Chocolate Cheesecake
Amherst Shore Country Inn
Shell:

1 cup graham cracker crumbs	250 mL
4 tbsp cocoa	60 mL
2 tbsp sugar	30 mL
4 tbsp unsalted butter, melted	60 mL

Filling:

1 lb cream cheese, softened	500 g
1/2 cup superfine sugar	125 mL
3 large eggs	3
1 cup sour cream	250 mL
8 oz semisweet chocolate, melted and cooled	250 g
1 tsp vanilla	5 mL
1 tsp almond extract	5 mL
1/3 cup Amaretto	75 mL

Topping:

2 oz semisweet chocolate	60 g
2 tbsp unsalted butter	30 mL
1/2 cup heavy cream, well chilled	125 mL
1 tbsp icing sugar	15 mL
2 tsp Amaretto	10 mL
1/4 cup toasted almonds, sliced	50 mL

To prepare the shell, combine the graham cracker crumbs, cocoa, sugar and butter in a bowl. Press the mixture into the bottom and 1 inch up the sides of a 10-inch (25-cm) springform pan.

To prepare the filling, beat the cream cheese with the sugar in a bowl until the mixture is smooth. Beat in the eggs, one at a time, beating well after each addition. Stir in the sour cream, chocolate, vanilla, almond extract and Amaretto. Turn the mixture into the shell and bake in a preheated 300°F (150 degree C) oven for 1 hour. Turn the oven off and let the cheesecake cool in the oven for 1 hour. Let the cheesecake cool completely on a rack and chill, covered loosely, for at least 12 hours.

To prepare the topping, in the top of a double boiler set over barely simmering water, melt the chocolate and stir in the butter. Spread the mixture over the cheesecake and chill for 1 hour. In a chilled bowl, beat the cream with the icing sugar and Amaretto until it holds stiff peaks. Pipe the cream onto the cheesecake and sprinkle with almonds.

Snow Pudding
Inverary Inn

1 tbsp gelatin	15 mL
1/4 cup cold water	50 mL
1 cup boiling water	250 mL
1 cup sugar	250 mL
1/4 cup lemon juice	50 mL
2-3 egg whites	2-3
Zest of 1 lemon	

Lemon Sauce:	
3 egg yolks, well beaten	3
1/3 cup sugar	75 mL
1/3 cup butter, melted	75 mL
2 tbsp lemon juice	30 mL
1 tbsp lemon zest	15 mL
1/3 cup heavy cream	75 mL

Soak gelatin in cold water for 5 minutes. Add boiling water and stir to dissolve. Add sugar and lemon juice. Place in the refrigerator until partially set, about 2 hours. Remove from the refrigerator and beat until frothy.

In a separate bowl, beat egg whites until stiff. Add lemon zest. Stir in gelatin mixture and refrigerate several hours, until set. Serve with lemon sauce. Serves 4 to 6.

To prepare lemon sauce, beat egg yolks, sugar, butter, lemon juice and zest. In a separate bowl whip cream and carefully fold in the lemon mixture. Chill and serve on Snow Pudding.

INNS
AND
RESTAURANTS

Amherst Shore Country Inn

Donna and Jim Laceby's Amherst Shore Country Inn is located at Lorneville, Cumberland County. The inn is just 25 miles (about 40 km) from the New Brunswick border and offers a panoramic view of the Northumberland Strait.

The inn has five bedrooms and serves complete gourmet dinners each evening at one sitting. Reservations are requested. The Amherst Shore Country Inn is open year-round. Further information can be obtained by writing to R.R. 2 Amherst, N.S. B4H 3X9 or phoning (902) 667-4800.

Bayberry House

Bayberry House, in the village of Granville Ferry, overlooks the Annapolis River Basin and is one mile (about 1 1/2 km) from historic Annapolis Royal.

Built in 1893 by Joseph Mills, an Annapolis Royal merchant, this Victorian home is furnished almost entirely in Georgian-period antiques.

Owned and operated as a bed and breakfast by Aileen Adams and Anne Wanstall, Bayberry House also offers dining to its resident guests by advance reservations.

Open year-round, the inn offers three bedrooms with a shared bath. Information can be obtained by writing Box 114, Granville Ferry, N.S. B0S 1K0 or phoning (902) 532-2272.

Blomidon Inn

Situated in the university town of Wolfville in Nova Scotia's Annapolis Valley, the Victorian-styled Blomidon Inn was built in 1877 by Captain Rufus Burgess, a local shipping entrepreneur. Burgess directed his captains to bring exotic timber as ballast on their return voyages. These woods were used to create the entrance hall and stairway of the inn.

The inn, now owned by Peter and Gale Hastings, has 21 bedrooms, all decorated with antiques. Quilts and accessories have been handcrafted by Mrs. Hastings.

Breakfast is served for their guests, and lunch and dinner are open to the public. Reservations are advised. Further information can be obtained at 127 Main Street, Wolfville, N.S. B0P 1X0 or (902) 542-9326.

Blue Heron Inn

Built around 1880, The Blue Heron Inn has served as a church manse, a private dwelling and, in the 1930s, as the Old Elm Lodge. Completely renovated and decorated with antiques, it now serves as an inn, offering five bedrooms, two sitting rooms and a tearoom.

Located at Pugwash, 30 miles (about 48 km) east of Amherst on the provincial Sunrise Trail, the Blue Heron is near fishing, hunting, salt-water beaches, golfing and boating.

The inn is open June 1st through October 1st and at other times by request. The dining room is open June 15th to September 15th. Innkeepers John Caraberis and Bonnie Bond can be contacted through P.O. Box 405, Pugwash, N.S. B0K 1L0 or by phoning (902) 243-2900.

Boscawen Inn

Boscawen Inn is a restored Victorian mansion that is situated within the town of Lunenburg and overlooks its front harbour. The home was a dowry gift to Edna Rudolph from her father, Senator H.A.N. Kaulbeck, in 1888.

Today the inn offers guests 18 bedrooms that range from alcoves to large rooms furnished with canopy or four-poster beds.

The dining room is open daily and breakfast, lunch and candlelight dinner are served to the inn's guests and visitors. Innkeeper Leslie Langille welcomes you May through October at P.O. Box 1343 Lunenburg, N.S. B0J 2C0 or (902) 634-3325.

The Bright House

Historic Sherbrooke Village on Nova Scotia's eastern shore is the home of The Bright House. Built in 1850, this large frame building with clapboard siding was opened to the public as a dining room in 1974.

Operators Gordon and Wynneth Turnbull offer their guests country dining. Specialties include roast of beef with Yorkshire pudding, seafood casseroles and homemade breads and desserts. Baked goods are available from their bakeshop, located behind the dining room.

The Bright House is open from 11:30 a.m. to 9:00 p.m., June through October. For reservations phone (902) 522-2691.

The Cape House Inn

Country dining is offered at the restored settler's homestead, The Cape House Inn. Situated on a hill, the inn overlooks Mahone Bay and the surrounding countryside.

Hosts Ann and Ray Caverzan serve luncheon and English cream tea daily, except Mondays, June to October. Dinner is served Friday, Saturday and Sunday evenings. Dinner seatings are at 6:00 p.m. and 8:15 p.m.; reservations are recommended. Inquiries can be directed to R.R. 2 Mahone Bay, N.S. B0J 2E0 or (902) 624-8211.

The Captain's House

Originally known as "Shoreham," The Captain's House of Chester was built in 1822 by a New Englander, Rev. John Secombe. The building has changed hands many times, but is now restored as a restaurant.

Open seasonally, The Captain's House specializes in early Maritime cooking. Luncheon and dinner are served daily, and reservations can be made by calling (902) 275-3501.

Clipper Cay

Clipper Cay, located on the waterfront in Halifax's Historic Properties, offers a tableside view of harbour activity.

While seafood is the highlight of the menu, steaks and other entrées are also available. Clipper Cay is open 12:30 p.m. to 2:30 p.m. and 5 p.m. to 10 p.m., Monday to Friday; 5 p.m. to 10 p.m., Saturday. Reservations can be made by phoning (902) 423-6818.

Compass Rose

The Compass Rose is located in the centre of the town of Lunenburg, close to shopping and sightseeing, and is a short walk from the harbourfront.

Originally built in 1825 as a Georgian-style home with hipped roof, the structure has since undergone several renovations. In the late 1800s, the building was Victorian-ized: its traditional six-over-six windows were replaced by two-over-two windows and an Italianate frontispiece was added. The interior retains the proportions of the Georgian era, with ornamental archways and fireplace surrounds.

Hosts Suzanne and Rodger Pike operate the Compass Rose year-round as a restaurant, bed and breakfast inn and antique shop. Inquiries can be directed to P.O. Box 1267, Lunenburg, N.S. B0J 2C0 or (902) 634-8509.

Dublin Bay House

Recently constructed by hosts Bel and M.E. Voegelin, the Dublin Bay House is located at Dublin Shore, Lunenburg County. The restaurant overlooks the La Have Islands, Dublin Bay and the La Have River.

The specialty of the house is seafood, and great care is given to its freshness and preparation. The restaurant is open daily May through September, except Monday. Service Tuesday through Saturday is from 5:00 p.m. to 9:00 p.m. and on Sunday from 3:00 p.m. to 8:00 p.m. Reservations are recommended and can be made by calling (902) 688-2751.

Garrison House Inn

The Garrison House is a restored heritage property in Annapolis Royal, which, founded in 1605 by Samuel de Champlain, is Canada's oldest permanent settlement. The town and its environs offer museums, live theatre, historic gardens, golfing and touring.

The Garrison House, owned by Patrick and Anna Redgrave, features seven period rooms. A licensed dining room serves breakfast to guests only, and lunch, English cream teas and dinner to guests and visitors. Write 350 St. George Street, Annapolis Royal, N.S. B0S 1A0 or phone (902) 532-5750.

Gowrie

Gowrie

The Gowrie was constructed in 1830 for Mr. Archibald, the first Agent General of the General Mining Association, and was named by his melancholy wife after her home, Blair Gowrie, in Scotland. Homesick though they may have been, the Archibalds became permanent Canadians and maintained the home until 1975, when it was purchased by the present owner, Clifford Matthews.

The Gowrie is being restored in a 19th-century style and has six guest rooms at present. Breakfast and dinner are available for guests, and visitors are welcome, with advance reservations, at the 7:30 p.m. single-seating dinner. A second dining room is available for small groups and parties. Contact Clifford Matthews at 139 Shore Road, Sydney Mines, N.S. B1V 1A6 or (902) 736-9424.

Gramma's House

Gramma's House is located in the village of Port Saxon on Nova Scotia's south shore, midway between Shelburne and Barrington — a one-hour drive from the Canada-U.S. ferry terminal at Yarmouth.

Built in the 19th century by the present owner's great-grandfather, the house offers guests overnight accommodations with breakfast. The Tea Room is open from noon to 5:00 p.m., and dinner is served from 5:00 p.m. to 7:00 p.m. (reservations please).

All meals are prepared by the owner, Jean Turner, and a local chef. The inn offers four bedrooms and operates seasonally, June to October. Additional information can be obtained by writing R.R. 3, Shelburne, N.S. B0T 1W0 or phoning (902) 637-2058.

The Grand

Fashionable Spring Garden Place in Halifax, with its collection of boutiques, shops and markets, is the site of The Grand restaurant. Aptly named, this restaurant offers a bar, a main dining room and The Rainbow Grill, for informal, lighter meals. Patrons are treated nightly to music played on a restored 1906 grand piano.

Cuisinier Bernard Meyer features French cuisine. The Grill and bar are open daily from 11:30 a.m., and the dining room serves dinner nightly. Reservations can be made by contacting general manager Gerard Breissan, 5640 Spring Garden Road, Halifax, N.S. at (902) 421-1116.

Harris' Seafood Restaurant

Harris' Seafood Restaurant is entering its thirty-third year of operation. Owned and operated seasonally, June to September, by Charlie and Clara Harris, the restaurant features homemade breads, a salad bar, seafood, beef entrées and desserts.

Harris' is located at Dayton, a few miles east of Yarmouth on route 1. For reservations, phone (902) 742-5420.

Highland Heights Inn

Highland Heights Inn

"Ciad mile failte," the Gaelic greeting of "one hundred thousand welcomes," aptly describes the atmosphere of Highland Heights Inn and the village of Iona.

Centrally located on Cape Breton Island, the inn is adjacent to the Historic Highland Village, a museum devoted to the life of early Scottish settlers.

The inn offers 26 rooms with full bath and is operated seasonally, May 1st to October 31st. Inquiries can be directed to Scott MacAuley at R.R. 2 Iona, N.S. B0A 1L0 or to (902) 622-2360.

INN
BEAR
RIVER

Inn Bear River

Inn Bear River, as its name implies, is found in the village of Bear River, the "Switzerland" of Nova Scotia. Founded in the 18th century by lumbermen and shipbuilders, Bear River is noted today for its craftsmen, who are drawn to the area by its beauty and casual lifestyle.

Built 95 years ago by shipbuilder Aldolphous Marshall, this 15-room Gothic Revival home was known locally as "The Millionaire's House." Nancy Onysko and Doug Dockrill operate the inn year-round and can be contacted at P.O. Box 142, Bear River, Annapolis Co., N.S. B0S 1B0 or (902) 467-3809.

Inverary Inn

A touch of Scotland is found at Inverary Inn in Cape Breton. Situated at Baddeck, with private lake frontage on Bras d'Or Lake, the inn features 25 rooms, seven cottages and The Patch Quilt Gift Shop. The dining room serves such specialties as bannock, Scottish oatcakes and desserts to guests and visitors. The season is from May 1st to November 1st. Innkeepers Dan and Isabel MacAulay can be reached by writing Baddeck, N.S. B0E 1B0 or phoning (902) 295-2674.

Keltic Lodge

"My dear, that is the place!" So spoke Henry Corson in the late 1800s on first viewing Middle Head, the present site of Keltic Lodge. The Corsons, from Akron, Ohio, had been advised to find a healthier environment for Mrs. Corson, who had tuberculosis. Within the year Middle Head was purchased, a large log home built, orchards planted and a thriving dairy farm established.

Today the Corsons' home has been replaced by the main lodge at Keltic, but the ocean, the mountains and the clear, unpolluted air still identify it as "the place" the Corsons saw nearly a hundred years ago.

Keltic Lodge is now operated by the Province of Nova Scotia. From mid-December to the end of March, the White Birch Inn and Cape Smokey offer lodging and gourmet dining. The complete complex is open from June to mid-October and offers convention services, salt-water pool, tennis courts, championship golf course, lodging and European cuisine. Inquiries can be made by writing Ingonish Beach, N.S. B0C 1L0 or by telephoning (902) 285-2880.

L' Auberge   *L'Auberge*

L' Auberge is an older-style hotel located at 80 Front Street, Pictou, and offers the public year-round service with its 20 rooms and dining room.

One of Nova Scotia's founding towns, Pictou was settled by six families from Pennsylvania and Maryland, who had been sent there by the Philadelphia Company. Six years later, in 1783, the ship Hector arrived, bringing the first Scottish Highland settlers to Canada. Scottish immigrants began to pour into this area, which was so like their native land, creating the strong Scottish cultural heritage that is still evident in the province today.

Innkeepers Josette and Pierre Poidevin specialize in French cuisine and seafood. Inquiries can be directed to P.O. Box 99, Pictou, N.S. B0K 1H0 or to (902) 485-6367.

Lobster Treat

Once an old schoolhouse, the Lobster Treat, located at 241 Post Road, Antigonish, features seafood and an assortment of entrées.

Jim and George Lerikos are the hosts at the Lobster Treat, which is open daily from 11:00 a.m. to 11:00 p.m. For reservations, phone (902) 863-5465.

The Manor Inn

Ted Pitman is the host at The Manor Inn, which is located on Doctor's Lake, just minutes from Yarmouth.

The former estate of Commodore H.H. Raymond, the inn is a colonial structure surrounded by four acres of gardens.

The Manor Inn features nine bedrooms decorated with antiques, plus a dining room and English lounge. An additional 20 rooms are available on the property in the Lakeside Motel.

The inn is open year-round. Direct inquiries to P.O. Box 56, Hebron, N.S. B0W 1X0 or to (902) 742-2487.

Milford House

Milford House has been offering food, lodging and a peaceful retreat for outdoor enthusiasts since the 1860s. Built original- ly as a "halfway house for travellers," the inn was operated by the Thomas family until 1969. At that time it was acquired by a group of former guests who were dedicated to continu- ing the management of Milford House in its previous manner and to preserving its 600 acres of woodland.

Open from mid-June to mid-September, Milford House features 25 lakefront cottages, each with a private dock and all within walking distance of the dining room, which is located in the main lodge. Nature trails, canoe rentals, tennis courts, swim- ming, fishing and a children's play area are offered. Additional information can be obtained from propriewo.. Warren and Margaret Miller at R.R. 4 Annapolis Royal, N.S. B0S 1A0 or at (902) 532-2617.

The Moorings

Bill and Vina Percy have opened their 19th-century water-front home to guests, where they offer British-style "bed and breakfast" hospitality.

Located in Granville Ferry, one mile (about 1 1/2 km) from historic Annapolis Royal and four miles (about 6 1/2 km) from The Port Royal Habitation, Canada's oldest settlement, The Moorings offers accommodations and full or light breakfast from May 1st to September 30th. Evening dinner is served on request. Further inquiries can be directed to Box 47, Granville Ferry, N.S. B0S 1A0 or to (902) 532-2146.

The Mug Up

The term "mug up" denotes a snack or a bite to eat while aboard a fishing vessel. While it is not intended to be a full meal, it is meant to tide you over until the cook prepares the main meal.

True to its name, The Mug Up at 128 Montague St., Lunenburg, offers homemade chowders, chili, pies, cookies — all "tide-you-overs."

Proprietors Audrey Pittman and Judy Strong serve breakfast, lunch and light dinners daily from 8 a.m. to 7 p.m., May 15th to October 31st. From November 1st to May 14th, open hours are from 8 a.m. to 3 p.m. Inquiries can be made by calling (902) 634-3118.

The Normaway Inn

Nestled in the Margaree Valley of the Cape Breton Highlands, the Normaway Inn, with its 250 acres of open fields and woodlands, was built in 1928.

The inn offers nine bedrooms and a common living room with a fireplace. As well as the main lodge, there are six cottages and 11 chalets. Meals are served in the dining room, where you will be treated to country cooking with a touch of the gourmet.

The Normaway Inn offers its guests tennis courts, bicycles, hiking trails and live entertainment. Canoe rentals, fresh- and salt-water swimming and salmon fishing are found nearby.

The inn is open from June 15th to October 15th. Further inquiries can be made to innkeeper David MacDonald at Margaree Valley, Cape Breton, N.S. B0E 2C0 or at (902) 248-2987.

O' Carroll's

O'Carroll's

O'Carroll's, located at 1860 Upper Water Street, is in the heart of Halifax's restored waterfront district.

Host Jim O'Carroll brings years of experience in the restaurant business from Glasgow, Scotland, and offers patrons classic dishes with a variety of Scottish specialties. O'Carroll's is open for lunch from 11:30 a.m. to 2:30 p.m., Monday through Saturday, and serves brunch Sundays, from 11:00 a.m. to 2:30 p.m. Dinner is served nightly from 5:00 p.m. to 10:00 p.m. Reservations can be made by phoning (902) 423-4405.

The Pines Resort Hotel

The Pines is situated on a hill overlooking the beautiful Annapolis Basin, a short distance from the Digby-St. John ferry terminal. Originally operated by Canadian Pacific Railways, the complex is now one of three provincially operated resorts.

Accommodations are available in the main lodge and cottages. The Pines offers tennis courts, a championship golf course, heated pool, shuffleboard and croquet. The dining room serves continental cuisine, and dress regulations are in effect for dinner.

The Pines is open seasonally, mid-May to mid-October. Inquiries can be directed to P.O. Box 70, Digby, N.S. B0V 1A0 or to (902) 245-2511.

The Rope Loft

The Rope Loft dining room is situated on a restored wharf overlooking the front harbour in Chester. Host Peter Gowans offers dining in the restaurant's upper-level dining room and adjacent balcony, as well as facilities for large groups or tours on the lower level.

The Rope Loft provides mooring for yachts and is open daily from 12 noon to 10 p.m., May to October. For reservations, phone (902) 275-3430.

Silver Spoon Savouries & Desserts

The Silver Spoon Savouries & Desserts restaurant is located at 1865 Hollis Street, Historic Properties, in Halifax.

Owner Deanna Silver serves a wide variety of dishes, available to restaurant patrons or as a take-out. Specialties include homemade pasta, pâtés, truffles and a variety of cheesecakes, tortes and other desserts. Party trays, picnic baskets and gift items can be assembled on short notice.

Restaurant hours are Monday to Thursday, 11:30 a.m. to 11:00 p.m.; Friday and Saturday, 11:30 a.m. to 11:30 p.m. Phone (902) 422-1510 or 422-1519.

Upper Deck Restaurant

If the stone walls could speak, tales of the turning tides of history would be revealed at the Upper Deck, Privateers' Warehouse, Halifax.

Once the home of Enos Collins, the warehouse housed the spoils of war, including in 1813 the booty from the famed Chesapeake and Shannon encounter.

Fully restored, the Upper Deck Restaurant offers a Maritime menu six days a week from 5:30 p.m. to 11:00 p.m. Reservations are recommended. Phone (902) 422-1289.

The Village Estate

The Village Estate

The Village Estate is a 19th-century Victorian mansion located at 164 Farnham Road, Truro, N.S. Built in 1870, "the mansion," as it was known by local residents, remained a family home, changing hands only a few times during the past century. With the exception of minor alterations in kitchen design, no structural changes have been made.

Restaurateurs Myrna and Mel Jordan serve steaks and seafood daily from 5:00 p.m. to 11:00 p.m. Reservations can be made by phoning (902) 895-3809.

The Whitman Inn

The Whitman Inn is a restored 1910 homestead located at Kempt, 2 1/2 miles (about 4 km) north of Kejimkujik National Park and halfway between Annapolis Royal and Liverpool.

Innkeepers Bruce and Nancy Gurnham offer guests accommodations and home-style breakfasts and dinners. Box lunches for hikers and canoeists are available upon request.

The Whitman Inn is open year-round. Inquiries can be directed to R.R. 2 Caledonia, Queens Co., N.S. B0T 1B0 or to (902) 242-2226.

The Zwicker Inn

The Zwicker Inn is owned and operated by Jack and Katherine Sorenson. Originally known as Zwicker's Inn or Tavern, and then as Zwicker's Hotel, this posthouse has been in operation sporadically since 1800. Lord Dalhousie, Lieutenant Governor of Nova Scotia in 1816 and later Governor General of the Canadas and Commander-in-Chief in India, recalled in his personal journal the frequent sojourns of his family to Prince's Harbour, the present Mahone Bay. The country tavern and inn kept by a German settler, Mr. Zwicker, became the focal point of their visits.

The Sorensons reestablished Zwicker Inn in 1980 as a restaurant offering Nova Scotian food. Soups, sauces, breads, noodles and ice creams are all made in their kitchen from fresh produce, meats and seafood.

Located at 662 Main Street, Mahone Bay, The Zwicker Inn is open year-round from 12 noon to 9 p.m. daily. For reservations, phone (902) 624-8045.

Index